D0947266

Rise and Fight Again

LIVES OF THE FOUNDERS

EDITED BY JOSIAH BUNTING III

ALSO IN SERIES:

FORGOTTEN FOUNDER, DRUNKEN PROPHET:
THE LIFE OF LUTHER MARTIN
Bill Kauffman

AN INCAUTIOUS MAN: THE LIFE OF GOUVERNEUR MORRIS
Melanie Randolph Miller

RISE AND FIGHT AGAIN

The Life of Nathanael Greene

Spencer C. Tucker

Wilmington, Delaware

Tucker, Spencer C., 1937–

Rise and fight again : the life of Nathanael Greene / Spencer C. Tucker.
—1st ed. —Wilmington, Del. : ISI Books, c2009.

p. ; cm.
(Lives of the founders)
ISBN: 978-1-935191-15-5
Includes bibliographical references and index.

1. Greene, Nathanael, 1742–1786. 2. United States—History—Revolution, 1775–1783. 3. United States. Continental Army—Biography. 4. Generals—United States—Biography. I. Title. II. Title: Life of Nathanael Greene. III. Series.

E207.G9 T83 2009 2008939576
973.33/092—dc22 0904

ISI Books
Intercollegiate Studies Institute
3901 Centerville Road
Wilmington, DE 19807-0431
www.isibooks.org

Manufactured in the United States of America

To Becky Snyder

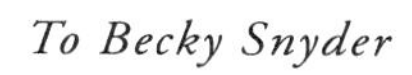

Nathl Greene

Major General United States Army

FROM THE ORIGINAL PICTURE BY CHAPPEL IN THE POSSESSION OF THE PUBLISHERS.

Johnson, Fry & Co. Publishers, N.Y.

CONTENTS

PREFACE

NEXT ONLY TO CONTINENTAL ARMY COMMANDER GENERAL George Washington, Nathanael Greene was the ablest American general of the War for Independence. Historian Edward Lengel, in his study of George Washington's military career, speaks for many when he sums up Greene as "the youngest and most capable of Washington's generals." Although he acquired his knowledge of the military arts almost entirely from books and on-the-job experience, Greene proved extraordinarily capable. Although he won few battles, his campaign that won the South for the revolutionary cause is generally acclaimed to have been the most brilliant and daring of the entire war.

A strict disciplinarian who insisted on "spit and polish" and rigorous training, Greene was also deeply concerned for the welfare of his men. Hardworking and seemingly indifferent to fatigue himself, Greene was by nature a problem solver who understood people. As with Washington, he could recognize talent and knew how to utilize it effectively. By nature optimistic, Greene was also extraordinarily ambitious, sensitive, and proud. Probably because he had not been close to his own father and because he and Washington were very much alike, Greene absolutely worshiped the commander in chief as a father figure and accorded him his complete loyalty.

Despite his near-total lack of military experience, circumstances fortunate for the American nation in 1775 combined to raise the thirty-two-year-old Greene from relative obscurity to military prominence. A Rhode Island merchant and businessman by profession, he knew little of the military but applied sound leadership principles to become the youngest general in the Continental Army. Advancing from brigadier general to major general, Greene was considered by many of his contemporaries to be the ablest brigade and then division commander in the army. Certainly Washington placed great trust in him and, at a particularly difficult time for the army, assigned him the critical yet herculean task of serving as quartermaster general. Greene proved extraordinarily effective in this demanding assignment, as he did in all others.

In October 1780, Washington assigned Greene by far his most demanding task: command of the army's Southern Department. It was a command that Greene had actively sought. Taking charge of a sharply depleted, dispirited force lacking all manner of military equipment and even clothing, Greene refused to be drawn into pitched battles save on favorable terms. Rebuilding the Southern Army in less than a year, Greene adopted daring tactics that defied conventional military wisdom but that recaptured from British control most of the Carolinas and Georgia. Although Greene lost the most important of his Southern battles, that of Guilford Court

House, this sanguinary struggle led British Lieutenant General Charles Lord Cornwallis to withdraw with the bulk of his army into Virginia, which set up the Battle of Yorktown, the climactic engagement of the war.

Greene has rarely been accorded his earned place in American military history. This is in part explained by his early and unexpected death in 1786 at only forty-three. Fortunately, the popular perception of Greene is changing, thanks to the appearance of a number of new studies of the general during the last decade. These have served to give him his proper place in American military history.

I was delighted when Josiah Bunting approached me to write this book, for I have long admired Greene and welcomed the chance to learn more about him. It has been both a pleasurable and educational experience. Certainly I come away from it with an even greater appreciation of Greene's pivotal role in the Revolutionary War. I also believe strongly that lessons to be drawn from Greene's life transcend the Revolutionary War period, for the leadership principles he espoused have much to tell us today. The most important of these is that character, hard work, and common sense trump specialist knowledge.

The vast bulk of Greene's sizable personal correspondence survives, and for my primary sources I have relied mostly on the extraordinarily rich collection of the thirteen volumes of *The Papers of General Nathanael Greene*, compiled over a thirty-year span. *The Papers* contain letters from Greene to his wife Catharine (Caty) Greene. By all accounts quite lovely and flirtatious, Caty attracted the attention of many men. Unfortunately only his letters to her have been preserved. No doubt she herself destroyed her letters to him after his death, perhaps the result of Greene's unnecessary chiding about her writing skills and poor spelling. This short study, however, concentrates on Greene's military leadership and career. Because of space limitations, the only endnotes are those for direct quotations, which retain original spelling and punctuation. For consistency in casualty figures in battles, I have relied for the most part on Christopher Ward's *The War of the American Revolution.*

I am grateful to Larry Hoffman for his wonderful maps and to historians Jim Piecuch and Paul G. Pierpaoli, Jr., who have read and commented on the manuscript. My wife, Beverly Tucker, also read the work and provided insightful suggestions.

NATHANAEL GREENE TIMELINE

AUGUST 7 (JULY 27, OS), 1742	Born in Potowomut, in Warwick, Rhode Island
1768	Takes over operation of family foundry in Coventry
1771	Deputy to the Rhode Island Assembly
1774	Banished from the Quaker community for joining the Kentish Guards, the local militia
JULY 20, 1774	Marries Catharine Littlefield of Block Island
AUGUST 1774	Formation of Military Independent Company at East Greenwich
OCTOBER 27, 1774	Kentish Guards, local militia, chartered

May 8, 1775	Commissioned brigadier general of Rhode Island Army of Observation
June 22, 1775	Commissioned brigadier general in the Continental Army
August 9, 1776	Commissioned major general in the Continental Army.
March 2, 1778	Accepts position of quartermaster general of the Continental Army
July 26, 1780	Resigns as quartermaster general of the Continental Army
October 6, 1780	Appointed commander of West Point
October 14, 1780	Appointed commander of Southern Department of the Continental Army
December 2, 1780	Arrives at Charlottetown (Charlotte), North Carolina, to assume command of the Southern Army
March 15, 1781	Commands at the Battle of Guilford Court House
April 25, 1781	Commands at the Battle of Hobkirk's Hill
May 22–June 18, 1781	Commands at the siege of Ninety Six
September 8, 1781	Commands at the Battle of Eutaw Springs

December 14, 1782	Occupies Charleston after evacuation by British
November 1783	Leaves military service
August 1785	Retires to Mulberry Grove, Georgia
June 19, 1786	Dies at Mulberry Grove Plantation, Georgia

CHAPTER ONE

EARLY LIFE TO 1775

IN 1775 ON THE OUTBREAK OF THE REVOLUTIONARY WAR, Nathanael Greene seemed an unlikely candidate for a military career, let alone distinction as a brilliant strategist. Greene came from a decidedly unmilitary Quaker background and had no formal military training to speak of when he became a general in the Continental Army. Indeed, he suffered from a further liability in the form of physical disability: a slight limp. As an adult, he also was subject to severe bouts of asthma. Yet Greene and George Washington shared the distinction of being the only general officers to serve for the entire period of the Revolutionary War, and Greene rose to be one of the finest generals and influential leaders of the War for Independence. Although there is no proof of Washington having made such a designation, several of his key subordinates believed that Greene was his choice to succeed him should that prove necessary.

Greene was born into a prosperous Quaker family in Potowomut, Rhode Island, on August 7 (July 27 OS), 1742. Potowomut is an isolated neighborhood of Warwick and was originally a village in the Warwick Township of Kent County. It is located on a peninsula between Greenwich Bay to the north and Narragansett Bay to the south. Potowomut is about two miles east of the nearest large community of East Greenwich.

Greene's relatives had arrived in America a century before. In the early 1630s, John Greene, a religious dissident and surgeon by profession, left Salisbury, England, with his wife and five children for Massachusetts Bay. Greene was a follower of the charismatic Roger Williams, and when Williams was banished from the Bay Colony for his teachings, Greene went with him to help establish a new colony, known first as Providence and later as Rhode Island, on land purchased from the Wampanoag Indians. There John Greene became a Quaker.

John Greene's great-grandson was Nathanael Greene Sr. An astute businessman, he bought out his brothers' holdings and ultimately owned several forges and became known for the production of iron ship anchors. Greene also owned a gristmill and was the proprietor of a general store. His firm, Nathanael Greene & Co., became a prosperous enterprise, with Greene reportedly paying the second highest taxes in Warwick. Known as a hard worker, he also served as a part-time Quaker minister. The Greene family lived in a fine house that had been built by Nathanael Sr.'s father in 1684.

Nathanael Greene Sr. had a large family: two boys and a girl by a first marriage and six sons by his second wife, Mary Motte. His second son in his second marriage was Nathanael Greene Jr. Most of what we know of Nathanael Jr.'s youth comes from his grandson, George Washington Greene, who had the opportunity to meet with some of Nathanael's brothers and with people who knew him. George Washington Greene describes a childhood that mixed play in nearby woods with hard physical labor.

Nathanael's mother died when he was not yet eleven and seems not to have been a major influence on him. This was not the case with his father, however. Although he appears to have been both narrow-minded and stern, from all accounts the elder Greene also was fair. Nathanael Jr. wrote of him, "My Father was a man [of] great Piety, had an excellent understanding; and was goven'd in his conduct by Humanity and kind Benevolence."

At the same time, Nathanael Jr. and his father were very different. The senior Greene shared the Quaker belief that advanced education was not only unnecessary but might actually lead to immorality and heresy. This was a serious barrier to a boy who from an early age thrived on books and education. Greene expressed bitterness about this years later when he wrote: "My Father was a Man of Industry and brought up his Children to Business. Early very early when I should have been in the pursuit of Knowledge, I was digging into the Bowels of the Earth after Wealth. . . . His mind was over shadow'd with prejudices against Literary Accomplishments."

The elder Greene believed that the boys should be able to read and write sufficiently well and should master enough math to be able to engage in business. The Bible was the standard literary text of the day, and to complement it, the Greene boys read Quaker texts by founder George Fox, including one entitled *Instructions for Right Spelling and Plain Directions for Reading and Writing True English*, designed to instruct Quaker children in English grammar but also in Quaker theology. Greene also read another work by Fox, *The Journal*, as well as Robert Barclay's Quaker text, *An Apology for the True Christian Divinity.*

Young Nathanael's siblings apparently were content to follow the course set by their father, but Nathanael resented his father's strictures against education and was both sufficiently strong-willed and possessed of enough thirst for learning to pursue an education. Greene wrote: "I lament the want of a liberal Education; I feel the mist [of] ignorance to surround me, for my own part I was Educated a Quaker, and amongst the most Superstitious sort, and that of itself is a sufficient Obstacle to cramp the best of Geniuses, much more mine."

Apparently Nathanael did persuade his father to hire a tutor, Adam Maxwell, who had emigrated to Rhode Island from Scotland. Supposedly Maxwell was to instruct the boy in mathematics and Latin, but he or someone instilled in Nathanael a love of the classic Roman writers, for in not too many years Greene demonstrated a knowledge of works by Julius Caesar, Seneca, Horace, and Euclid. His brothers recalled seeing Nathanael late at night, book in hand, sitting on a stool and reading by firelight. He read whenever the opportunity presented itself, even, on occasion, while he was supposed to be working. When his father refused to buy books for his son, on his own time Nathanael fashioned small anchors and other toys to sell in Newport, New England's second busiest seaport, when he traveled there in the sloop *Two Brothers* with cargoes of anchors and flour. In Newport, Greene also did not hesitate to approach people who were better educated than he and from whom he could learn. These included the Reverend Ezra Stiles, later president of Yale College.

Nathanael was much interested in geometry, and reportedly his first purchase was a volume by Euclid. Other books included works by Seneca and Horace and by modern writers such as John Locke (*Essay on Human Understanding*) and Jonathan Swift.

Although Greene was largely self-taught, frequent recollections by contemporaries of his ability to hold his own in conversation suggest a man who was well educated according to the standards of the day.

Nathanael Greene Sr. did not interfere with this activity and might even have taken some secret pride in his son's enterprise. The elder Greene was, however, firmly opposed to Nathanael Jr.'s other great passion: dancing. On one occasion his father reportedly whipped him for sneaking out of the house at night to attend a dance. This punishment apparently did not deter the strong-willed Nathanael from continuing the activity. Throughout his life, he always enjoyed dancing and the company of the opposite sex. George Washington Greene related the story of how one dancing partner accused Greene of dancing "stiffly," no doubt in reference to his slightly lame right leg—a birth defect—to which Nathanael replied, "Very true, but you see that I dance strong."

Nathanael's older stepbrothers Benjamin and Thomas died in 1760, and a legal battle ensued over the inheritance. Nathanael, then only eighteen and the best-educated family member, took the lead in a successful effort to keep the family holdings together, preserving these for his father, himself, and his brothers Jacob, William, Elihu, Christopher, and Perry. In order to prepare himself for these legal proceedings, Nathanael read the classic work on English law, Sir William Blackstone's *Commentaries*. Although we know few details, apparently the case took him out of Rhode Island, to Connecticut, and New York City.

Nathanael Greene grew into a handsome, tall (5'10") young man. He was broad-shouldered and strong, no doubt partly due to his work at the forge. He had determined features and a firm mouth, high forehead, and blue-gray eyes. He had a slight blemish in his right eye, the consequence of an inoculation for smallpox during a trip to New York City. His decision to receive the inoculation, which was then illegal in Rhode Island, is yet another indication of his independent, rationalist spirit. He also was able to overcome his stiff knee. Barely noticeable, reportedly it did not prevent him from being able to outrun, outfight, and outdance most of his peers. In his twenties, however, he developed asthma that plagued him the remainder of his life.

Although he was very much involved in learning the family businesses, Greene also continued his interest in intellectual pursuits. This included a petition, which he probably wrote himself, to the Rhode Island Assembly, calling on it to relocate Rhode Island College from Warren to East Greenwich. Notwithstanding the petition's characterization of East Greenwich as "abounding with Every necessary supply to render the Scholars Comfortable," including a post office, Rhode Island College moved instead to Providence, where it became Brown University.

In November 1770 Greene Sr. died, and his surviving sons inherited his businesses, but Nathanael Greene Jr. was clearly the most important figure in these enterprises. Just before his father's death he had moved to Coventry, about ten miles west of East Greenwich, where the family had established a new foundry. There he built a new eight-room house, which he called Spell Hall. This residence contained a library to house his growing collection of books.

Greene was now a community leader. Reportedly he took charge of the effort to establish the first public school in Coventry. Although no doubt he engaged in conversations during his frequent business trips to Newport about the implications of the English Parliament's efforts to tax its American colonies, there is no indication during this period of Greene's involvement in radical political activity. Greene's lengthy correspondence in the early 1770s with Samuel Ward Jr., who in 1771 at age fourteen was already a student at Rhode Island College, is entirely devoid of such discussions.

Greene did continue his self-education. For whatever reason, this activity was now directed more toward military topics. Greene noted later that he read, in addition to Caesar's narratives of his campaigns, writings by Prussian King Frederick II ("the Great"), including his *Instructions to His Generals*, and French Marshal Maurice de Saxe's memoirs, *Mes Reveries.*

After moving to Coventry, Greene fell in love with Anna Ward, daughter of Samuel Ward and older sister of Samuel Ward Jr. Anna's father was one of the important political leaders of Rhode Island and on occasion its governor. Greene was crushed when in the summer of 1771 she rejected his marriage proposal.

Two years later, however, in 1773, at a dance in East Greenwich, Greene again fell in love, this time with Catharine Littlefield. Caty, as she was known to her friends, was an orphan and ward of Greene's cousin, William Greene. She has been described as slight of build, witty, and a graceful dancer. Although, like her suitor, limited in formal education, Caty was bright and clever. Flirtatious, she clearly enjoyed the company of men. Caty immediately captured Greene's affections. On July 20, 1774, the two were married in East Greenwich in a small ceremony. He was a few days shy of thirty-two, and she was but nineteen. They were a perfect match: he was solid and dependable; she was vivacious and charming.

Now apparently settled into a business career, Greene brought Caty back to Coventry, intent on amassing a fortune and starting a family. Theirs was largely a very happy and satisfying union, but they were not to enjoy matrimonial bliss for long. The gathering storm clouds over New England were about to break into open rebellion.

CHAPTER TWO

THE APPROACH OF WAR

SEPARATED BY THREE THOUSAND MILES OF OCEAN AND DISSIMilar circumstances, it was inevitable that differences in outlook would arise between the ruling class in Britain and the inhabitants of British North America. Statesmen in London did not understand this, and, even when they did, they made little or no effort to reconcile the differences. The communities on each side of the Atlantic had been growing apart for some time, but the crushing British victory over France in the French and Indian War of 1754–63, known in Europe as the Seven Years' War of 1756–63, actually worked against British rule. The removal of the French threat gave free play to the forces working for separation. Although the war had been won largely by British regulars, Americans magnified their own role in the victory; in any case, the colonials believed that their contributions to it diminished their obligations to Britain.

Almost immediately after the war, in 1763 Chief Pontiac of the Ottawa Indians led an intertribal alliance in a rebellion along the western frontier. British regulars put it down, but in these circumstances, London decided to station 10,000 regulars along the frontier and have the Americans pay part of their upkeep. The plan seemed fair, especially as the mother country was hard-pressed for funds following the heavy expenditures of the French and Indian War, and because the soldiers would be protecting the colonials both from Indian attack and any French resurgence. This decision, however, ignited a long controversy about Parliament's right to tax.

The question became: what taxes would the Americans be willing to pay? Americans—that is, those apart from slaves and indentured servants—were probably the freest people in the world. Apart from import duties (many of which were evaded through widespread smuggling), Americans paid only those few taxes assessed by their own colonial legislatures.

Parliament's effort began with the American Duties Act of April 1764, commonly referred to as the Sugar Act. Although it lowered the duty on foreign molasses, it imposed the duty on all sugar or molasses, regardless of its source. The act also insured that the duty would be paid, and it established a new vice-admiralty court with jurisdiction over customs cases in the British colonies, placing it in the garrison town of Halifax, Nova Scotia, where British judges presumably would be safe from intimidation.

The Sugar Act aroused great resentment among the colonists. James Otis of Massachusetts denounced the new act in his pamphlet *The Rights of the British Colonies Asserted and Proved.* This work enunciated the principle of no taxation without representation. The Sugar Act hit Rhode Island hard, for that colony's economic fortunes were closely tied to the rum trade. There was thus considerable anger when the British warships *Squirrel* and *Maid-*

stone were sent to Newport to enforce the act. In late 1764, Rhode Island Governor Stephen Hopkins published a treatise, *The Rights of the Colonies Examined*, in which he inveighed against both the Sugar Act and another new tax, the Stamp Act. Parliament, he claimed, had no right to collect taxes without the consent of the colonists themselves.

The Stamp Act of 1765 was a levy on all paper products. Such a tax was not new and was in widespread use in Europe. A cargo of the stamps arrived at Newport aboard a British ship that October, but opposition to the tax was so strong that the stamps were not unloaded. The act was repealed the next year. Generally unnoticed in the excitement over the repeal was the Declaratory Act of March 1766. It asserted Parliament's right to bind its American colonies "in all cases whatsoever."

The next effort by Parliament to find some tax that the colonials would pay came in the Townshend Acts of 1767. These imposed customs duties on glass, lead, paint, paper, china earthenware, silk, and tea imported from Britain into the colonies. According to Chancellor of the Exchequer Charles Townshend, the revenues raised would be applied to help pay the salaries of royal governors and judges, as well as the cost of defending the colonies. But the act was clearly an attempt to make British officials independent of colonial legislatures to enable them to enforce parliamentary authority. After colonial protests, in March 1770 this act too was repealed, save for the tax on tea.

Tensions between colonists and British soldiers also had been rising. This was in part for economic reasons; many British soldiers had, out of need, taken part-time jobs away from Bostonians. Another problem was the Quartering Act, by which Bostonians were forced to house and feed British troops. These factors led to a bloody confrontation on March 5, 1770: the so-called Boston Massacre.

Rhode Island was in the thick of these developments. On May 16, 1769, angry Rhode Islanders at Providence tarred and feathered several customs officials. Then on July 19, 1770, the British customs schooner *Liberty* arrived at Newport to enforce the customs laws and prevent smuggling. Its captain, determined to do his duty, had fired on a suspicious colonial vessel—no doubt a smuggler—the day before. A large crowd of angry citizens gathered on the wharf, confronted the captain, and instructed him to order his crew ashore. Members of the crowd then boarded the ship and burned it.

Greene, meanwhile, had become more politically active. In 1771, he won election to the Rhode Island General Assembly, serving there until 1775 and rewriting the colony's militia laws. He also soon became involved in what became a famous incident in the path to revolution.

In early 1772, the sixty-foot British revenue schooner *Gaspee*, purchased by the British government in North America, arrived in Newport to enforce the revenue acts. Its captain, Lieutenant William Dudingston, was well aware of what had happened to the *Liberty* but nonetheless was determined to do his duty. His ship stopped every colonial vessel entering or leaving Newport and subjected it to a thorough search for contraband.

On February 17, Dudingston ordered his crew to search the merchant ship *Fortune* in Newport Harbor. It had a cargo of fourteen hundred gallons of rum and forty gallons of "Jamaican Spirits." Rufus Greene, a cousin of Nathanael Greene, was at the helm, and the *Fortune* was owned by none other than Nathanael Greene & Co. Dudingston apparently handled young Rufus Greene roughly and ordered the *Fortune* towed to Boston where its future could be decided by an admiralty court rather than being adjudicated by a local jury at Newport, which might be expected to find for the ship owners.

Greene was outraged at the news. He wrote that he was setting out in pursuit of a "Searover" (i.e. a pirate) who had made off with "a quantity of our Rum and carried it round to Boston. . . ." The "illegallity of [the] measure created such a Spirit of Resentment That I have devoted almost the whole of my Time in devising and carrying into execution measures for the recovery of my Property and punishing the offender."

Indeed, Greene brought a lawsuit against Dudingston, demanding compensation, and the case became a cause célèbre in Rhode Island. The lawsuit forced Dudingston to evade the colony's officials, who were authorized to arrest him. Meanwhile, Dudingston continued aggressive enforcement of the law, creating no little havoc at Newport and causing Governor Joseph Wanton to complain to Dudingston's commanding officer, Admiral John Montagu, at Boston, but to no avail. The exchange between Montagu and Wanton was terse. Montagu warned Wanton that he had heard rumors of plans in Newport to fit out a vessel that might then attempt to cut out ships seized for illegal trading activity. Were this to occur, Montagu warned, the guilty parties would be hanged as pirates. Wanton replied that he did not take instructions from "the King's Admiral stationed in America."

Much to the chagrin of Newport merchants, that summer Dudingston continued his rigid enforcement of British law. On June 9, 1772, the *Gaspee* fired a shot across the bow of the merchant ship *Hannah* in Narragansett Bay. Benjamin Lindsay, captain of the *Hannah*, attempted to escape, and Dudingston ordered the

Gaspee to give chase, but Lindsey took his own ship into shallow water and there the *Gapsee* promptly grounded. Lindsey then sailed his own ship on to Providence some six miles distant and reported what had transpired.

Late that night, more than sixty men set out in a half dozen longboats from Providence. The crew of the *Gaspee* spotted the approach of the longboats, and Dudingston appeared on deck with a pistol and demanded to know who the men were. Sheriff of Kent County Abraham Whipple identified himself and said that he had a warrant for Dudingston's arrest in connection with Greene's lawsuit. Whipple demanded that Dudingston surrender, but he refused and was shot in the groin. The Providence men then boarded the revenue schooner and overpowered its crew, transporting them to shore before returning to torch the *Gaspee*.

The *Gaspee* Affair caused a sensation. British officials in London, even King George III, were outraged. Lord Hillsborough, British secretary of state for American affairs, resigned. The king ordered a royal commission to investigate the crime and bring those responsible to justice. Meanwhile, Governor Wanton was obliged to issue a proclamation offering a reward of £100 for information on the perpetrators. George III personally raised the reward to £500. Despite this considerable sum and the commission of inquiry, no one came forward.

Indeed, the Kent County sheriff arrested Dudingston in his hospital bed, allowing the trial against him for his seizure of Greene's ship to proceed, and Greene ultimately won a judgment against the lieutenant of some £300, although there is no indication that he ever received the money. Certainly Greene & Co. desperately needed the funds, because even as the case was being argued, in August 1772 the forge at Coventry was destroyed in a fire, plunging Greene into despair and bringing on an acute attack of asthma.

The *Gaspee* Affair was certainly a major event in Greene's life. Suggestions that he was among the perpetrators carried considerable personal risk, for suspects, once apprehended, were to be transported to England for trial. This grave personal threat seems to have awakened in Greene a political outlook heretofore lacking. His extant earlier correspondence makes no mention even of the Boston Massacre, but after the *Gaspee* Affair, it is laced with references to British tyranny and the threats posed by the crown to colonial liberties. Thus, Greene wrote Samuel Ward Jr. that while witnesses could establish his complete innocence in the affair, the investigatory commission was "justly Alarming to every Virtuous Mind and Lover of Liberty in America." He also condemned the Rhode Island General Assembly for not protesting the work of the commission as "betrayers of the Peoples Liberties." Greene saw in his own difficulties the fate of all Americans. Whatever his motivations, Greene had become a patriot.

Matters were now coming to a head between the Crown and colonial agitators. The prolonged British effort to bring the colonies to heel, and colonial resistance to it, ended with the so-called Boston Tea Party. In May 1773, Parliament attempted to rescue the financially strapped yet politically well-connected British East India Company. The government authorized it to sell its considerable surplus of tea directly to its own agents in America. The tea would actually be cheaper, even with the tax in place, than smuggled Dutch tea, but the arrangement would cut out colonial middlemen, establishing a monopoly on what was the principal colonial drink and ending a major element of the smuggling trade. Public meetings in New York, Philadelphia, and Boston all condemned the act.

At the end of November 1773, three ships carrying East India Company tea arrived at Boston. Two mass meetings at that port demanded that it be returned to England without payment of duty. With no action forthcoming, on the evening of December 16, some eight thousand people met in protest, and afterward a number of them, roughly disguised as Mohawk Indians, boarded the tea ships and, working throughout the night, emptied them of 342 large chests of tea, which were dumped into Boston harbor. Further disorders against the landing of tea followed in other American seaports.

This event ended the period of British government patience. Frustrated by its fruitless decade-long effort to tax the colonies and by colonial intransigence and lawlessness, London now adopted a hard line. Determined to teach the rebellious American subjects a lesson, in March 1774 King George III and his ministers pushed through Parliament the first of what became known as the Coercive Acts, measures known in America as the Intolerable Acts. The first of these, the Boston Port Bill, closed the port of Boston, threatening the colony with economic ruin. Other legislation suspended the charter of Massachusetts, placed that colony under martial law, and gave the new government extensive new powers over town meetings. A Quartering Act required colonial authorities to provide housing and supplies for British troops. If the colonists would make restitution for the destroyed tea, the restrictions would be lifted. Nonetheless, this strong action against a colonial government and the colony's economic livelihood created a firestorm in America, lending credence to arguments by the New England radical leaders that the British were out to crush American liberties.

At the same time, although not part of the coercive program, the Quebec Act of May 1774 seemed a gratuitous British insult and one of the "intolerable" measures. Actually one of the most enlightened pieces of imperial legislation of its day, it sought to reconcile the large number of French Catholics to British rule by granting full civil rights and religious freedom to Canadians. This was anathema to many Protestants in New England. More importantly for the seaboard colonies, it defined the borders of the former New France as the French had drawn them, cutting the colonies off from further westward expansion.

After the Intolerable Acts and the Quebec Act, self-authorized groups met in several colonies and sent delegates to a "Continental Congress" in Philadelphia in September 1774. It adopted the so-called Association that called for nonimportation of English goods after December 1. Individual colonies then organized committees of public safety, and Greene's brother Jacob was a member of the Rhode Island committee.

Greene followed these events closely. Boston was only sixty miles from Coventry, and he made frequent business trips there. On one of these trips Greene met bookseller Henry Knox. The two men soon became fast friends and often discussed events and their common belief of inevitable war between Britain and the colonies. The two shared an interest in military science, and both sought to prepare themselves for the coming conflict through independent study. Knox, the future commander of the Continental Army's artillery, read everything he could on that subject, while Greene read the writings of French Marshal Henri de la Tour d'Auvergne, Vicomte de Turenne. Through Knox, Greene met Samuel Adams and Paul Revere.

Greene now firmly identified with the radicals. His language and outlook as expressed in his correspondence was fully as extreme as their own. Thus, in a letter to Samuel Ward Jr., Greene charged that the British ministry in London

> seems to be determined to embrace their cursed hands in American Blood, and that once Wise and Virtuous Parliament, but now Wicked and weak Assembly, lends an assisting hand to accomplish their hellish schemes. The soldiers in Boston are insolent above measure. Soon very soon expect to hear the thirsty Earth drinking in the warm Blood of American sons. O how my eyes flashes with indignation and my boosom burns with holy resentment.

Greene joined others in raising funds to buy food to assist the people of Boston. He contributed 2£ 8S, the second highest sum among eighty citizens who signed a subscription deploring the "Late, Cruel, malignant and more than savage Acts of the British Parliament."

Increasingly, Greene also involved himself in militia activities. In August 1774, he helped found a militia company in East Greenwich, one of a number of such companies being organized throughout the colonies, and especially New England, in direct response to events in Boston. Tradition has it that on one of his trips to Boston, Greene, assisted by Knox, hired a deserting British Army sergeant to go to East Greenwich and drill the new unit, known as the Kentish Guards (for Kent County), several times a week. Greene also purchased a musket in Boston and smuggled it out of the city, and he enlisted in the new unit as a private. On October 29, 1774, the Kentish Guards were accepted by the Rhode Island Assembly as a recognized state military unit. Writing to a friend, Colonel James Varnum, at the end of October 1774, Greene explained his support for a militia unit in these words: "I thought the cause of Liberty was in danger and as it was attackt by a military force it was necessary to cultivate a military spirit amongst this People, that should tyranny endeavor to make any further advances we might be prepared to check it in its first sallies."

While some writers have claimed that it was this military activity that caused Greene to be read out of the Quakers, recent scholarship suggests otherwise. Greene was already drifting away from the family religion and indeed had become cynical about organized religion in general. Part of it was resentment over the claims of religious leaders to be the guardians of public morals, and indeed the action that led to his departure from the Quakers was having been seen with a cousin at "a Place in Coneticut of Publick Resort [i.e. tavern] where they had No Proper Business."

While some members of the Kentish Guards wanted Greene as that unit's first lieutenant, apparently a majority objected to his slight limp, believing that officers should not suffer from physical disability and that such would reflect poorly on the unit as a whole. This was a great blow. Attorney Michael Varnum, one of Greene's close friends, had accepted the captaincy of the unit, and, angry at the treatment of Greene, he reportedly threatened to resign his commission. Greene wrote Varnum on October 31: "Let me intreat you Sir if you have any regard for me not to forsake the company at this critical season, for I fear the consequences. . . . I would not have the company break and disband. . . . It would be a disgrace upon the county and upon the town in particular." At the same time, Greene was deeply wounded. He noted that he had been told that he "was a blemish to the company." He admitted that "it is my misfortune to limp a little but I did not conceive it to be great. . . . I had pleased my self with the thoughts of serving under you, but as it is the general Opinion that I am unfit for such an undertaking

I shall desist. I feel not the less inclination to promote the good of the Company because I am not to be one of its members. I shall do every thing in my power to procure the Charter." Greene did not resign; indeed, he became one of the company's most faithful members, drilling with it regularly.

Meanwhile, by the winter of 1774–75, North America was a powder keg. British commander in North America Lieutenant General Thomas Gage reported to London that the situation was dangerous and that he lacked sufficient manpower to deal with events if fighting were to break out. This did not influence George III and his ministers, who were determined to pursue a hard line. In February 1775 Parliament declared Massachusetts to be in rebellion.

Gage strongly disagreed with London's approach. In a report sent to London but not shared with Parliament, he estimated that, in the event of fighting, it would take a year or two and 20,000 men just to pacify New England. If these men could not be supplied, Gage advocated a naval blockade and economic pressure as the best approach. London disagreed. The ministry held that 10,000 troops, supported by Loyalists, would be sufficient. Surely Gage was a defeatist or worse. London believed that the vast majority of Americans were loyal to the crown, that any problems were the work of only a few agitators, that a show of force and the arrest of the troublemakers would restore order, and that all would then be well.

The war that London now entered into so blithely caught Britain unprepared. Troops would have to be raised, the navy rebuilt, and men and supplies shipped across the ocean. While the Royal Navy, once rebuilt, could land troops at any point on the American seaboard and extract them again, campaigning in the interior in a land without adequate roads or strategic centers would be difficult indeed.

Fighting began on April 19, 1775, when Gage sent troops from Boston to destroy stores of arms that the radicals had been stockpiling at Concord. He had successfully carried out similar operations in the past, but this time the militia were alerted. At Lexington, Gage's troops encountered a hastily assembled small militia force, and, in a skirmish, easily brushed them aside. The British then marched on to Concord and completed their mission. The withdrawal to Boston became a nightmare, however, for the local militia was by then out in full force, and they sniped at the British from cover along the route. In all, the operation claimed 273 British casualties of some 1,800 engaged (73 killed, 174 wounded, and 26 missing) and 95 Americans (49 killed, 41 wounded, and 5 missing). Militia forces then closed around Boston, opening a siege. The War for American Independence had begun.

Mounted couriers spread the news, and Greene learned of events that same day. He bid a hasty goodbye to Caty and marched with the Kentish Guards for Providence, fourteen miles distant. The royalist governor of Rhode Island ordered the Kentish Guards to return home, but Greene, two of his brothers, and several other men rode on toward Boston to assess the situation, only returning when they learned that the British troops had all returned there.

Several days later, the General Assembly of Rhode Island selected Greene as one of two commissioners to meet with Connecticut representatives concerning common defense measures. At the same time, the General Assembly ordered the raising of a brigade of 1,500 men, known as the Army of Observation. On May 8, after two other men had turned down the post, Connecticut officials named Greene a brigadier general and commander of the

Army of Observation. This decision set in motion everything that followed.

The selection of Greene to head Rhode Island's military effort appears surprising, given that his sole military experience consisted of six months' occasional drill as a private in the Kentish Guards. Yet Greene was hardly unknown. He had established political connections and had served in the assembly. The decision was most probably based on Greene's brief show of leadership as one of the commissioners treating with Connecticut and on his fixity of purpose and apparent appetite for command. Greene's commission called on him to "resist, expel, kill and destroy" any enemies who might invade or assault America, "in Order to preserve the interest of His Majesty and His good subjects in these parts."

Greene's brother Jacob now assumed direction of the family's financial enterprises, while both Nathanael and his brother Christopher went off to war. (Christopher, then a colonel, was killed in fighting in May 1781 at Croton, New York.) Greene spent the next several weeks preparing the brigade for war. A stickler for details, he quickly became acquainted with his staff and key officers and drilled the men. He also busied himself securing supplies, and at the end of May 1775, the brigade set off for Roxbury near Boston. Caty, now pregnant with their first child, remained in Coventry.

CHAPTER THREE

BEGINNING OF THE WAR AND THE SIEGE OF BOSTON

BRITISH COMMANDER IN NORTH AMERICA AND GOVERNOR OF Massachusetts Lieutenant General Thomas Gage had long experience in North America. He also knew that the resources available to him were totally insufficient for the task at hand. Gage could not mount even a limited offensive until June, and even then he received only 3,500 men. As so often occurs, both sides seriously miscalculated the costs and duration of the war, but Gage had a better sense than most of the enormity of the task facing Britain. He warned London, "The rebels are not the despicable rabble too many have supposed them to be." The war ahead would be difficult, as the Americans "never showed so much conduct, attention and perseverance as they do now."

Massachusetts General Artemas Ward assumed command of the Patriot forces ringing Boston. On May 23, 1775, Greene met with Ward and placed his own men under Ward's command.

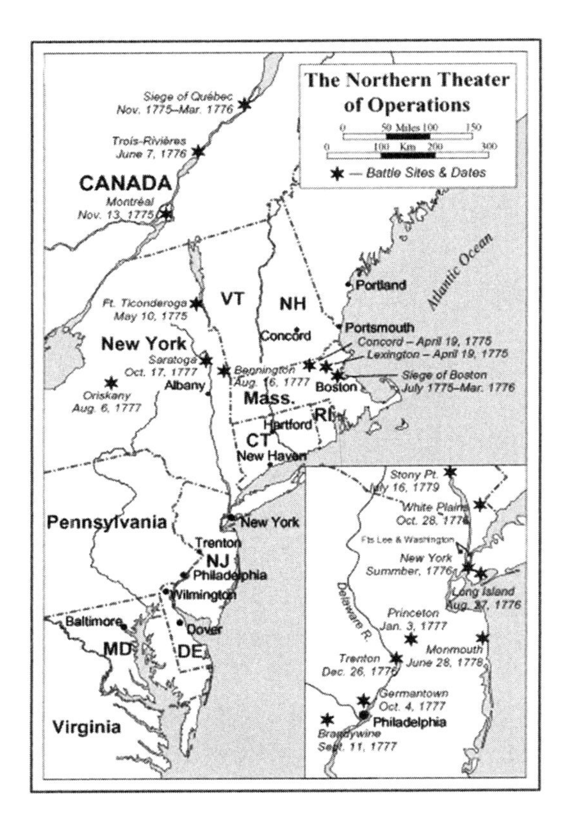

Technically, each colony fielded its own army, so Greene's gesture was an important one. Greene's Rhode Islanders took up station at Roxbury, Massachusetts, on the colonial right wing. Greene found an ideal bivouac for his troops on the sixty-acre estate of one-time Massachusetts governor Francis Bernard.

Clearly Greene believed wholeheartedly in the cause on which he had now embarked. He wrote to Caty on June 2: "It had been happy for me if I could have lived a private life in peace and plenty. . . ." But "the injury done my Country, and the Chains of Slavery forgeing for posterity, calls me fourth to defend our common rights and repel the bold invaders of the Sons of freedom. The cause is the cause of God and man." Greene concluded, "I am determined to defend my rights and maintain my freedom, or sell my life in the attempt. . . ."

Greene early demonstrated what came to be regarded as superlative leadership abilities. Although on occasion he traveled to confer with Rhode Island leaders in Providence in order to arrange for supplies, he spent much time training his men. He cared passionately about their welfare, and, as would be the case throughout the war, led by example. Greene was always up early and made frequent inspections. There was a great deal of administrative work, and Greene often worked late into the night on paperwork and correspondence. He wrote his brother Jacob on June 28: "My task is hard and my fatigue great."

Greene insisted that his officers always present the best appearance and would not allow soldiers without shoes on the parade ground. The hard work paid off, for the brigade's three regiments were soon recognized as the best disciplined and equipped of the colonial militias in the siege of Boston. Varnum assumed command of one of the regiments, and Christopher Greene was a major in the same unit.

Greene was in Coventry in mid-June on a brief leave to settle family affairs, which meant that he missed the Battle of Bunker Hill (Breed's Hill) on June 17, 1775. Three days before, the New England militias had moved into Charlestown Peninsula north of Boston, which was dominated by Breed's and Bunker Hills. On June 16, the Americans occupied Bunker Hill, the highest ground and a favorable position as long as the adjacent land and narrow escape route could be held. They also occupied Breed's Hill, which was closer to Charlestown, lower, and more vulnerable to a flanking attack.

On June 17, British troops under Major General William Howe crossed over to Charlestown and mounted a frontal assault on the colonial positions. Although the militias eventually broke and ran, this came only after they had repulsed three British assaults and exacted a frightful toll of the advancing British soldiers. In terms of percentage of force engaged, Bunker Hill was one of the most sanguinary battles of the entire century. Its effects remained with Howe and may well have contributed to his failure, when British commander in chief, to press home subsequent assaults. Howe wrote, "When I look at the consequences of [the battle], in the loss of so many brave Officers, I do it with horror. The Success is too dearly bought."

Learning of events from a courier on June 18, Greene immediately left Coventry, but he arrived to find the battle over and Charlestown a smoking ruin. He then busied himself preparing his men for a possible British move against the Patriot right. The British had indeed planned an attack on Dorchester Heights to the south of Jamaica Plains, but they called it off after the bloodletting of Breed's Hill. Greene took from the battle the lesson that largely untrained troops, properly led and entrenched, could indeed inflict heavy casualties on a well-trained attacking force. He wrote his brother Jacob, "I wish [we] could Sell them another Hill at the same Price we did Bunkers Hill."

Obviously, the colonies now required some sort of regular military establishment, and on June 14, 1775, the Continental Congress authorized the formation of ten rifle companies. This was the first regiment and is generally regarded as the beginning date for the U.S. Army. The next day, June 15, Congress appointed forty-three-year-old Virginian George Washington as commander in chief of the Continental Army, or the Army of the United Colonies as it was usually referred to even as late as 1783.

Washington had served in the Virginia militia. His first rank was that of major at age twenty-one, on the eve of the French and Indian War, but he failed in his efforts to dislodge the French from Fort Duquesne in an action that in fact began the French and Indian War. Washington had then served as a volunteer aide to British Major General Edward Braddock in the latter's disastrous 1755 expedition against Fort Duquesne, and had been recognized for his bravery under fire and good work in helping to bring off British survivors of the French and Indian attack. He then trained and headed a Virginia regiment as a militia colonel. While there were others with more military experience—notably Charles Lee and Horatio Gates—Washington was native born and was from Virginia, an important political asset. He also actively sought the position of commander in chief, appearing at sessions of the Continental Congress in his militia uniform. His selection by Congress proved fortuitous.

In addition to Washington, the new army was to have four major generals (in order of rank: Artemas Ward, Charles Lee, Philip Schuyler, and Israel Putnam) and eight brigadier generals. Greene was one of these and last in rank. At age thirty-two, he was the youngest of the eight. His date of rank was June 22.

Washington arrived at Cambridge on July 2 and immediately assumed command. Two days later, Greene sent an officer with a letter of welcome and two hundred picked men from his brigade. Washington was impressed with the appearance of the men, and shortly after they returned, a letter arrived from him inviting Greene to a personal meeting. Despite the fact that the two men seemed to be quite different—Washington aloof and patrician, Greene direct and eager to please—the two men were almost instantly drawn to each other, and a close relationship developed that would have a profound impact on the course of the war. From the beginning, Greene respected Washington both as a leader and a military commander, and gave him his unswerving loyalty.

On his part, Washington, a keen judge of men and of character, sensed in Greene qualities that he admired. These were loyalty, respect for authority, fixity of purpose, a strong sense of honor, and frankness in opinion. Washington also appreciated Greene's reputation as a strict disciplinarian who was nonetheless also even-handed and fair, and he must have been impressed by the obvious confidence of the Rhode Island soldiers in Greene's leadership.

Washington and Greene were in fact very much alike in many respects. Perhaps Washington saw in Greene something of himself. He also was largely self-educated and had learned much of the military art by reading. The two men were also similar in temperament. Like Washington, Greene on occasion had trouble controlling his temper. Greene also saw the older Washington as something of a father figure. As evidence of this admiration, Greene named his first child, a son, George Washington Greene.

Much of Greene's time was consumed with matters of supply. In early July, Greene's men were outraged to learn that a shipment of "beef" was actually horsemeat, and on July 4 Greene condemned a supply of moldy bread that had arrived from Providence. Greene wrote to Governor Cooke, "[I am] willing to spend and be spent in so Righteous a Cause, but unless I am supported by the helping hand of Government, my endeavors will be defeated and your expectations blasted." Greene noted, "If the Troops are comfortably subsisted, if they don't do their duty, they can be punisht with great justice, but if they are not well fed and properly clad, they excuse all their misconduct from one or the other Reasons."

Washington also had his hands full, and not only with matters of supply and discipline. Squabbling among his officers was rife, and units from one colony looked askance at those from another and refused to serve under officers from other colonies. Washington had wanted to break down the provincial barriers entirely by forming the men into fully integrated divisions. As Greene noted in a letter to Ward, "His Excellency has a great desire to Bannish every Idea of Local Attachments." Greene agreed with Washington on this issue, noting, "For my own part I feel the cause and not the place. I would soon go to Virginia as stay here." Strong objections to the plan forced Washington to back down, however. Local preference remained strong, and regiments continued to be organized by colonies until the end of the war.

Washington soon gave Greene command of a Continental Army brigade of seven regiments: his own three Rhode Island regiments and four from Massachusetts. Greene then redeployed from Roxbury to Prospect Hill, north of Cambridge. There he came under the direct command of left-wing commander Major General Charles Lee.

Lee remains a controversial figure. Born in England and the same age as Washington, he had far better military credentials than the Virginian, for Lee had actively served as a British Army officer in America in the French and Indian War and in Portugal. He had also spent time in Poland, where he was made an honorary major general, and he had observed fighting during the Russo-Turkish War. Rising to lieutenant colonel in the British

Army but believing that the crown had accumulated too much power, Lee sailed for America in 1773. Lee strongly believed that he, not Washington, should have been named commander of the Continental Army, and he actively competed with Washington for the loyalty of the men. He also urged guerrilla warfare, a strategy Washington rejected.

There was, meanwhile, little action during the siege of Boston. Both sides continued to improve their defenses, and occasional shelling and sniping occurred between Continental riflemen and the British where the opposing lines were close enough to allow. The Continental Army continued to train, but the men and their leaders knew of or cared little for proper field sanitation, and Greene reported to Governor Cooke in early August, "Our Troops are now very sickly with the Dysentery." Conditions were not much better in Boston where, with half its normal population, there had been an outbreak of smallpox and morale was low among the British troops, with attendant desertions.

In late 1775, however, Washington and Greene and other Continental Army generals faced a formidable obstacle: enlistments of the New England soldiers were to expire on December 1, whereupon the inadequately supported army would largely disband. Washington's dire statements to Congress about the situation finally brought to Cambridge a congressional delegation of Benjamin Franklin, Benjamin Harrison, and Thomas Lynch. The three arrived on October 18 and remained four days, during which they received a steady stream of complaints. The army was about to go home, Washington said, and Congress would then have to recruit a new army, or the siege of Boston would end, and the British would have won. The commissioners also heard detailed expositions on such subjects as the supply situation, pay, uniforms, and rations. The commissioners then returned to Philadelphia and conveyed to Congress what they had learned.

Washington's dire predictions bore fruit in a reorganization of the Continental Army. The army was to consist of 20,000 men in twenty-six regiments, and Congress authorized Washington to recruit new soldiers to serve one-year enlistments, to expire on December 31, 1776. Greene and other generals urged Washington to call for the granting of bounties to soldiers then in uniform who reenlisted, but the commander in chief rejected this sound approach, which was also opposed by many in Congress. Part of this was a naiveté regarding the military. The revolutionaries saw themselves engaged in an entirely just cause and superior to the British in virtue. As such, they believed they must also be superior in innate military prowess. The war would thus be of short duration, and all that was required was good generals to lead virtuous men. The fighting would be shared, with everyone taking their turn. Such naiveté almost led to ruin. Most recruits were in their late teens or early twenties and were usually poor and unmarried and for the most part untrained. In contrast to many on the British side, they were willing soldiers, but they were facing perhaps one of the world's best-trained and most disciplined armies.

Greene's predictions were borne out. Not only was it now harder to recruit new men, but most of the soldiers and even officers did not reenlist. Of sixteen second lieutenants in Greene's two regiments, not one reenlisted. Few came forward to fill the Rhode Island quota of 1,500 men. Greene wrote to Samuel Ward Sr., then a member of Congress, to praise the Massachusetts men, but despaired over the attitude of his own colony: "I was in hopes then that ours would not have deserted the cause of their Country. But they seem to be so sick of this way of life, and so home sick that I fear the greater part and the best part of the Troops from our Colony will go home. . . . I fear the Colony of Rhode Island is upon the decline. . . . No Publick Spirit prevails."

In the fall of 1775, Gage returned to England, and Howe took command of some 8,000 British troops. With Continental Army enlistments about to run out, there was great pressure on Washington to act and, as was his habit throughout the conflict, he called a council of war. It met at his headquarters at Cambridge on October 18 to discuss whether to mount an attack. Washington had first raised the issue a month before. In the company of other officers who had the military experience he himself lacked, Greene did not hesitate to speak his mind. All the other generals thought an attack too risky and opposed it. Only Greene favored it, although he qualified this to the extent of supporting an attack only if 10,000 men could be landed in Boston.

Washington's reaction to the position taken by his most junior general is unknown, but he sided with the majority: the Continental Army remained in its defensive positions around Boston. In February 1776, when Washington again raised the issue, Greene was more cautious and, in a letter to Jacob Greene, remembered his position in October differently. While still supporting an attack, he characterized an assault on 8,000 entrenched regular troops as "a serious object" and claimed that he had said that "I always thought that an attack with 20,000 men might succeed." Continental Army strength before Boston was then about 18,000 men.

If Greene changed his mind, it was because he was learning the profession of arms. His good friend General Henry Knox, commander of the Continental Army artillery, said of Greene: "[He] came to us the rawest, the most untutored being I ever met with." In less than a year, however, Greene "was equal, in military knowledge, to any General officer in the army, and very superior to most of them."

The winter was difficult on the men conducting the siege, with very cold weather and even firewood scarce. In December 1775, Greene noted that some of the men were "Obligd to Eat their Provision Raw for want of firing to Cook. . . . Our suffering has been inconceivable."

Greene was an early advocate of independence. He declared openly, even before the beginning of fighting, that the colonies would have to set up their own government. And since September 1775, he had been outspoken on the issue of independence, although he was willing to continue a "connexion" with Britain, if its "tyrannical measures" were ended and American freedom preserved. "But," he wrote prophetically, "I had rather continue in the field seven years than submit to their tyrannical measures." In October 1775, he wrote to Samuel Ward Sr. that the issue was clear: "A separation from Great Britain or subjugation to her." Greene urged Ward and Congress to seek an alliance with France against Britain: "We want not their Land Forces in America; their Navy we do." In the meantime, the French government was correct "in refusing to intermediate" until there were "no hopes of accommodations between us and Great Britain." In December 1775, he wrote his brother Jacob, "We are now driven to the necessity of making a declaration of independence. We can no longer preserve our freedom and continue the connection with her [Britain.]"

In January 1776, Greene wrote again to Ward at Philadelphia, "Permit me to recommend from the sincerity of my Heart . . . a declaration of independence." He assumed France and Spain had both made offers of assistance. "Let us embrace them like Brothers." But only a declaration of independence, Greene believed, would lead France and Spain to assist the colonies with their navies. With France and Britain at war, Britain would have to turn its attention to Europe and defense of its vulnerable German possession of Hannover."

In the military reorganization that followed the Cambridge meeting, Greene's three Rhode Island regiments became the new 9th and 10th Continentals. Yet Greene's predictions concerning the difficulty of recruitment without bounties were borne out, for at the end of the year, about 10,000 men had enlisted to serve another year in the Continental Army, only half the desired troop strength established by Congress. On December 31, 1775, Greene put the situation to Samuel Ward Sr.: "We never have been so weak as we shall be tomorrow when we dismiss the old Troops; we growing weaker and our Enemy growing stronger renders our situation disagreeable."

Greene, however, saw the new army that had taken the place of the old force of provincial militias as a significant step. He put it in these words: "We have just experienced the inconveniency of disbanding an Army within Cannon Shot of the Enemy and forming a new one in its stead, an Instance never before known. . . . A large Body of Troops Probably will be wanted for a considerable Time."

On January 1, 1776, however, Greene's brigade numbered only 700 men—fewer than half its authorized strength. Despite difficult conditions, Greene maintained tight discipline. Typically he spent his days with his men and then much of the night writing colleagues and friends. Greene also appealed to Washington for a leave to return to Coventry and visit the now very pregnant Caty, but Washington denied the request. Greene was required at Boston, which the commander in chief hoped to attack before spring when the British would surely reinforce. Hard work and fatigue now took their toll. Greene experienced stomach problems, and in late January he developed jaundice. He wrote his brother Jacob on February 8,

> I have got the jaundice, and I have been confined twelve or fourteen days. I am as yellow as saffron, my appetite all gone, and my flesh too. I am so weak that I can scarcely walk across the room. But I am in hopes I am getting something better. I am grievously mortified at my confinement, as this is a critical, and to appearance, will be an important period of the American war. Cambridge Bay is frozen over; if the weather continues a few days longer as cold as it has been some days past, it will open a passage into Boston. Sick or well, I intend to be there, if I am able to sit on horseback.

Learning of her husband's poor health, Caty, having in mid-February given birth to George Washington Greene, insisted on joining her husband. Other officers' wives were already in camp, including, since autumn, Martha Washington. Caty had been there once before, so she would not be shocked by what she found. Her arrival at the end of February was an immense balm to Greene, who apparently had already largely recovered. Washington was charmed by Caty, as were many other officers, and Caty and Mrs. Washington soon became fast friends.

The Continental Army also appeared to be recovering. Although the force was still largely untrained, by spring it numbered perhaps 18,000 men, including some 3,500 militia. These faced some 8,000 British troops in Boston. Although his generals remained opposed to an attack, Washington was determined to do something. On May 10, 1775, in a daring action, a small force under Colonels Ethan Allen and Benedict Arnold had seized some 120 British cannon and mortars at Fort Ticonderoga. The Americans went on to take the British forts at Crown Point and St. John's. During the winter of 1775–76, Washington's chief of artillery and Greene's good friend Henry Knox succeeded in bringing down a number of these captured guns from Ticonderoga. Hauled by oxen on sledges, fifty-nine of them arrived in the Boston area in early February.

Washington then proceeded to seize the high ground of Dorchester Heights that overlooked the British in Boston from the south. Fortunately for the Americans, Howe had made no effort to take and hold this vital high ground. Washington assumed that once the Americans were in possession of the heights, Howe would then have no choice but to attack, an option the American commander welcomed. Washington ordered Greene, Israel Putnam John Sullivan, and Horatio Gates to plan and carry out the operation. The Americans were to carry out a surprise occupation of the heights and complete the defensive fortifications in only one night. Because the ground was frozen, the soldiers prepared heavy wooden breastworks that could be strengthened with earth later. Barrels filled with earth would be rolled into place and wooden abatis installed.

To conceal his plans, on the night of March 2, Washington opened a heavy bombardment from Lechmere Point, Cobble Hill, and Roxbury. The cannonade resumed the next night, and the next. The British replied but little damage was done on either side. On the third night, March 4–5, however, 2,000 American troops occupied and fortified Dorchester Heights. By dawn on the fifth, the Americans were firmly entrenched and, with the cannon in place, could bombard the British at will.

Contrary to Washington's expectations, Howe was not preparing to attack but rather was planning to evacuate smallpox-infected Boston. Washington's move caused Howe to change his mind and prepare an attack, but a late winter storm led him to cancel it, and the presence of the cannon made the British situation untenable. Howe then began an evacuation to Halifax, which was completed two weeks later on March 17. An informal agreement was reached: Washington agreed not to harass the British with cannon fire as they evacuated, and Howe promised not to destroy the city. Washington entered Boston on March 18. Two days later, he named Greene its military governor. The first stage of the war had ended in an American victory.

CHAPTER FOUR

NEW YORK AND NEW JERSEY

AS MILITARY GOVERNOR OF BOSTON, GREENE APPLIED HIS considerable energies in an effort to restore the city to some degree of normalcy. He was determined that the Continental Army garrison would not be a burden to the weary, starving inhabitants who had already endured so much from the British. On March 27, 1776, Greene issued orders establishing firm rules for the occupying troops and promising swift punishment for any soldiers guilty of taking civilian possessions or even condoning such activities. "If any should be base enough to commit any Acts of Plunder and attempt to conceal the Effects, their messmates . . . will be considered as accessary to the Crime . . . and will be punished accordingly." Greene also condemned "Indecent language, it being ungenerous, unmanly and unsoldier like."

Greene was military governor of Boston for less than two weeks, for on March 29, Washington ordered him to march toward New

York on April 1 with a brigade of five regiments. The reason was obvious. Howe had sailed off with his army, but no doubt would soon regroup and make use of the Royal Navy's control of the sea to move against some other point along the Atlantic seacoast. New York City was the most obvious objective. It was probably the closest thing to a strategic center in America, and a British base there would enable them to move up the Hudson River, known at the time as the North River.

Washington was determined to hold New York. He had written Colonel William Alexander, known as Lord Stirling, who was charged with constructing defenses on Long Island: "It is the Place that we must use every Endeavour to keep from them. For should they get that Town, and the Command of the North River, they can stop the Intercourse between the northern and southern Colonies, upon which depends the Safety of America." Control of the North River would allow the British easy access to Canada and enable them to isolate New England, the font of the rebellion. Retaining New York, Washington believed, was of "infinite importance."

Greene echoed these sentiments. He had written Samuel Ward Sr. on January 4, 1776, that New York would certainly be the next British objective and should immediately be fortified. He noted New York's "Vast Importance to the Enemy" because of the North River and access to Canada. Maintaining Continental Army control of New York was vital to the "General success of our Arms."

Greene departed Boston on April 1, 1776, moving with his brigade overland. Caty was with him. On April 4, they were in Providence. The next day, Greene turned out his men to greet Washington, who passed through that city on his way to New York. Greene ordered that the men wash and be well groomed and that their uniforms be cleaned. The people of Providence cheered both Washington and Greene as they rode past. Greene delivered Caty to Coventry, then proceeded with his men to New London, Connecticut. From that point, the brigade traveled in ships under Continental Navy commander Commodore Esek Hopkins up Long Island Sound to Brooklyn, arriving there on April 17.

Washington demonstrated great confidence in Greene, assigning his youngest general the defense of Long Island. This was centered on Brooklyn Heights, a commanding topographical feature that rose some one hundred feet over the water and overlooked the East River to Manhattan Island and New York City itself. The Americans understood the importance of Dorchester Heights in reducing Boston. They did not want to see the British turn the tables in New York City.

On Long Island, Greene's brigade labored to complete the defensive works begun by Major General Charles Lee even before the fall of Boston and, following Lee's departure for the South, by Colonel Alexander, Lord Stirling. As completed, the zigzag American defensive line covered a distance of about one and a half miles across a peninsula from Gowanus Cover in the southwest to Wallabout Bay in the northeast. It included five forts, one of which was named Fort Greene, and a number of redoubts. In all, the positions mounted twenty-nine cannon. Behind the works lay Brooklyn, the East River, and, just beyond that on Manhattan Island, Washington's headquarters. There was a serious geographical drawback that Greene could not surmount, however. Long Island was surrounded by deep navigable water, and the British commanded the sea. The American 18-pounders at Red Hook, the extreme westerly position on the fortified peninsula, would be no match for the 32-pounder cannon carried by the Royal Navy's ships of the line.

During these months, Greene drew closer to Knox. Their two wives subsequently joined them in New York, and the four spent a number of evenings together at Knox's headquarters in the southern end of Manhattan. Caty Greene continued her friendship with Martha Washington. Twice Caty's age, Martha had first taken an interest in her during the siege of Boston. This friendship grew until June 1776, when Caty suddenly left New York on learning that her son was seriously ill. On her return to Rhode Island she was greeted with the good news of his recovery, and, missing both her husband and the excitement of New York, she soon returned to the city. She came back to a very different situation, for the British were about to invade.

The politically astute Greene also nurtured a relationship with one of the leaders of Congress, John Adams of Massachusetts. In the spring of 1776, Greene's good friend Samuel Ward Sr. had died of smallpox, cutting Greene off from access to Congress and a means of making his own views heard there. Never lacking in self-confidence, Greene did not hesitate to approach the intellectual Adams, who had graduated from Harvard and whom Greene had first met during the siege of Boston. The correspondence between the two men provides an interesting glimpse of the development of military policy and strategy. Thus Greene argued that military promotions ought to be the sole prerogative of Washington as commander in chief, while Adams replied that this authority properly rested with Congress. Their correspondence dealt with a wide range of military issues, including higher pay for officers and benefits for the families of men killed in service.

Greene also set about, not so subtly, to advance his own promotion to major general. Again, Greene's self-confidence and ambition show through. Although he was Washington's youngest brigadier general and had no military command experience before the war, Greene believed himself qualified for the higher rank. He also made not so subtle hints that unless he was advanced in rank, he might resign. Thus he wrote to Washington in late May 1776, "As I have no desire of quitting the service, I hope the Congress will take no measures that lay me under the disagreeable necessity of doing it."

Greene was not disappointed, for on August 1 he found himself one of the Continental Army's new major generals. Meanwhile, Greene had thrown himself into his work, not only supervising the finishing of the defensive works, but also attending to myriad logistical details and administrative concerns. With little staff assistance, Greene and other Continental Army officers, including Washington, had to do much of the day-to-day administrative work themselves. This ranged from signing passes to supervising courts-martial and writing frequent reports and requests to Washington. Greene did not shirk this responsibility and continued his practice of often working late into the night with little sleep. Somehow he also found time to keep up his extensive correspondence.

Throughout his military career, Greene understood the importance of maintaining the support of the civilian population. Thus, one of his orders came in response to local complaints and called on his men to end their practice of swimming nude in a nearby pond. His chief concern, however, was always for the well-being of his men. Good health was essential to maximize the number and efficiency of his force in combat. He believed that his men would benefit from eating more fruits and vegetables. He also emphasized the necessity of proper hygiene as including the frequent use of soap and the proper maintenance of latrines, and he ordered the men not to relieve themselves while in the fortifications.

Washington had ample time to prepare the New York defenses, for Howe took considerable time to prepare his next move. Not until June 1776 did Howe open the second phase of the war when he set sail from Halifax with 32,000 infantry in hundreds of transports convoyed by ten ships of the line and twenty frigates, all manned by 10,000 seamen. It was the largest expeditionary force in British history until the twentieth century. The advance elements of it arrived off New York on June 29, and on July 3, British troops began coming ashore on Staten Island. At the same time, another British force of 13,500 troops under British commander in Canada, Lieutenant General Sir Guy Carleton, was preparing to advance from the north down the Richelieu River-Lake Champlain invasion route.

To oppose Howe's force, Washington had at New York just 19,000 men. Not knowing where the British would strike, Washington had divided his men between Manhattan and Long Island. With the British amassing landing craft in the area, Washington feared that they would strike at both northern Manhattan Island and a second location simultaneously. In order not to be outflanked, Washington formed his men into five divisions, which he stationed in three major bodies: three divisions at the southern end of Manhattan Island; one near the northern end of Manhattan at Fort Washington, located on Mount Washington (today Washington Heights) on the Hudson River; and one on Long Island. Yet Washington placed his forces so far forward that they were in fact vulnerable to flanking attack. Although Howe mounted such attacks, he was too slow in pressing them home, and allowed Washington to escape each time.

Congress had made no provision for cavalry, and Washington likewise made no attempt to organize such a force on his own. He had available to him a regiment of 400–500 volunteers from

Connecticut, known as the "Light Dragoons," but did not think to make use of them and, indeed, sent them home. Even a small screening force might have prevented defeat.

On the evening of July 9, on Washington's orders, the New York troops gathered at their respective parade grounds, there to receive news of the Declaration of Independence, adopted by Congress a few days before in Philadelphia. The men cheered, and in New York's Bowling Green, a patriotic crowd toppled and destroyed a leaden statue of King George III.

Much to Washington's surprise, Howe was slow to act. At the beginning of August, Howe was reinforced by ships and men who had been repulsed on June 28 by General Charles Lee in the Battle of Sullivan's Island, near Charleston, South Carolina. Yet not until August 22, two months after his arrival, did Howe press his advantage and begin landing 20,000 men on Long Island.

Greene was not in command on Long Island when the British invaded. Over the previous several weeks, many of his men had fallen sick with what was probably typhoid. Greene himself was felled on August 15 and was confined to bed with a high fever and no energy. Although he informed Washington three days later that he was feeling somewhat better, the commander in chief would not risk having an ill Greene in command, for reports were rife that the British were making final preparations for their assault. He ordered Greene to cross to Manhattan and complete his recuperation there.

Washington replaced Greene with Brigadier General Israel Putnam, Greene's second-in-command. He then reconsidered his choice and named the more seasoned Major General John Sullivan, who was, however, ignorant of Greene's defensive plans. Washington also increased troop strength on Long Island from

4,000 to 9,000 men. By now Washington had at his disposal some 28,000 men, but many of these were untrained militiamen.

Greene was still recovering in a private residence in Greenwich Village, when the British attack occurred. On August 22, about 15,000 British troops landed on the southwest shore of Gravesend Bay without opposition. A long ridge ran east to west across the island. Known as the Heights of Guan, it was pierced by four passes. From west to east these were Gowanus Road, Flatbush Road, Bedford Pass, and Jamaica Pass. Howe feinted an attack against Flatbush Road and Bedford Pass, causing Sullivan to concentrate the bulk of his forces in these locations. On the night of August 26, Howe led the main body of some 10,000 men east in a wide movement in front of the American positions and through Jamaica Pass on the extreme Continental Army left, then moved west again, behind the American positions. With the British threatening to cut them off, the outnumbered Americans in Bedford Pass and Flatbush broke and fell back on the fortified Brooklyn Heights. At the same time, Major General James Grant led the remaining 5,000 British troops against the extreme right of the American line at the Gowanus Pass. Grant's job was to fix in place there some 1,600 Americans under Major General Alexander, Lord Stirling, until Howe could cut them off from the rear. To lull the Americans, Grant moved cautiously.

Putnam never did comprehend what the British were doing, and, as a result, in the Battle of Long Island on August 27, the Americans on the Gowanus Road were caught between two British forces nearly ten times their own number and were forced to surrender. Fearing disaster, Washington crossed the East River and took personal command of the American forces on Brooklyn Heights. The logical course was to extract his men, withdrawing them across the East River, but Washington was at first unwilling to consider it. Instead, he ordered reinforcements from Manhattan to Long Island, increasing his strength there to 9,500 men.

The British might now have taken a sizable part of the Continental Army and perhaps even its commander, but Howe shrank from the frontal assault on the American position on Brooklyn Heights that the Americans expected. No doubt Howe remembered what had happened at Breed's Hill. But Howe also did not make use of his naval power to cut the Americans off from escape. Instead, he ordered the digging of siege lines, no doubt expecting that Washington would recognize the hopelessness of his position and surrender. Heavy rains delayed the British preparations and also provided time for Washington to realize the precariousness of his situation. In consequence, in a brilliant operation, Washington ordered campfires kept burning and, on the night of August 29–30, thanks in part to heavy fog, brought all of his men and all but six of his cannon across the East River to Manhattan in boats manned by Marblehead, Massachusetts, fishermen. Washington was the last man on the last boat, leaving just as the British came up. The Americans suffered 1,012 casualties in the Long Island Campaign; British losses were but 392.

Greene knew the men and terrain far better than did Putnam and Sullivan and had believed that his soldiers, operating from behind fixed defenses, could turn back a British attack. No one can say what would have happened had Greene been in command, although it does seem unlikely that he would have ordered his men forward of their prepared defenses. The final outcome of the battle probably would have been the same. Greene admitted as much but lamented his inability to participate when he wrote to his brother Jacob on August 30:

> Gracious God! To be confined at such a time. And the misfortune is doubly great as there was no general officer who had made himself acquainted with the ground as perfectly as I had. I have not the vanity to think the event would have been otherwise had I been there, yet I think I could have given the commanding general a good deal of necessary information. Great events sometimes depend upon very little causes.

Greene was much alarmed by the general situation, in which the British could use their sea power to outflank the Americans on Manhattan Island by means of the Hudson and East Rivers. On September 5, he wrote Washington to urge "a General and speedy Retreat," which he believed to be "absolutely necessary and that the honour and Interest of America requires it. . . ." Without this, "Your Excellency will be reduced to that situation which every prudent General would wish to avoid; that is of being obliged to fight the Enemy to a disadvantage or Submit." Greene also favored a scorched-earth policy, including the burning of New York City and its suburbs. Two-thirds of the property, Greene claimed, belonged to the Tories. Destroying the buildings there would deny the British the opportunity to garrison their whole army in one place and "deprive them of a general Market. . . . And not one benefit can arise to us from its preservation that I can conceive of."

Greene advanced the same position in a council of war on September 7. He told the assembled officers that the army should not attempt to hold New York as Congress insisted. If American forces remained on Manhattan, the British would use their command of the sea to cut them off there. Greene urged a withdrawal to Harlem Heights and a stand there, retreating to Fort (Mount) Washington if need be. He believed that defending Manhattan would be a serious mistake. Nonetheless, the generals voted in favor of a compromise plan. As part of the plan, 9,000 men would move north to Harlem Heights in upper Manhattan, south of the strong point of Fort Washington on the high ground of the Hudson palisades. Another 5,000 troops would remain within the city, while a similarly sized force occupied positions between the two to guard against a British invasion from the East River.

Greene opposed this arrangement, which defended both everywhere and nowhere. Instead, he continued to push for a general withdrawal from Manhattan. Indeed, in what could be construed as a slap at the commander in chief, Greene sent a petition to Washington, begging for a new council of war to reconsider the plan. It was signed by six officers, with Greene the only major general.

The council of war met on September 11. Again, Greene spoke forcefully in favor of withdrawal, and this time he carried the vote. Washington apparently agreed with Greene on the destruction of New York, but he did not believe he had the authority to order this on his own. Meanwhile, on September 10, Congress had authorized Washington to withdraw from the city as soon as he thought it advisable. Following the council of war, the troops began moving north to Kings Bridge, while Washington transferred his headquarters to Harlem Heights. The decision came almost too late, however.

Fortunately, Howe delayed again. This may have been because of peace talks on Staten Island on September 11. The British emissaries offered no new proposals, whereas the American side, unaware of Washington's precarious situation, rejected concessions. The talks broke off without result, and Howe then moved.

On September 14, Howe sent four warships up the East River to Kip's Bay in eastern Manhattan. The next morning, 4,000 British troops crossed the East River from Long Island in flatboats to undertake an amphibious assault against the light American entrenchments at Kip's Bay. Fire from some seventy cannon aboard the ships supported the British assault.

The American withdrawal northward was not yet complete, and the British move threatened to cut off Putnam's division at the south end of the island in New York City from the remainder of the American army at Harlem Heights to the north. The American brigade at Kip's Bay broke and ran under the heavy but ineffectual British naval cannonade almost without firing a shot. Washington tried to rally the men and even struck soldiers and officers with his riding crop, but to no effect. Learning of these developments and short of wagons, Putnam was forced to abandon a large number of his heavy guns and supplies in New York City as he rapidly marched the twelve miles north to rejoin the main army at Harlem.

The next morning, September 16, saw the Americans in force at Harlem Heights. Greene and his 2,000-man division were situated just to the south. The battle began when the Americans opened up on a British light infantry unit of about 300 men advancing ahead of Howe's main army. The American troops fired several volleys at the British before moving northward. The British, confident of success and hoping to bag their opponents, unwisely pressed forward. Washington ordered Greene to send forward about 150 men to keep the British occupied, while sending a flanking force under Colonel Thomas Knowlton in an effort to cut off the attackers. The British spotted Knowlton before he could complete the encirclement, however, forcing the Americans to attack from the flank. Nonetheless, the British found themselves pressed between Greene's and Knowlton's forces, and, this time at least, they withdrew.

Washington declined to pursue, fearful of risking a general engagement. Harlem Heights was noteworthy as the first time that Greene had actively engaged in combat. He had shown considerable courage, riding among his men and shouting encouragement and orders. British losses may have been as high as 70 dead and 200 wounded, while Washington's losses included perhaps 30 killed and something less than 100 wounded and missing. Although the Battle of Harlem Heights was only a small affair, Washington's army had partly redeemed itself, and the battle helped restore the troops' confidence. The Americans had stood and fought at close range and had not withdrawn until ordered to do so.

Still, there was no denying that this small battle could hardly alter the outcome of the campaign for New York. Indeed, the next day Washington sent Greene across the Hudson to New Jersey in order to organize defenses there, including an earthen defensive work across the river from Fort Washington, at first known as Fort Constitution, and later renamed Fort Lee. A successful Continental Army defense of New Jersey was essential if the British were to be denied access to the interior and a march overland against Philadelphia. The task entrusted to Greene was an important one, but the commander in chief had full confidence in him. As Washington's secretary noted, "Greene is beyond doubt a first-rate military genius, and one in whose opinions the General places the utmost confidence."

Meanwhile, the wishes of Greene and Washington regarding an abandoned New York City came true to a considerable extent. On the night of September 20, a series of fires engulfed the city. Perhaps a third of New York burned.

Greene busied himself with strengthening Fort Lee. He supervised construction of a new barracks and improvement of the hospital facilities. Concurrent with his insistence on discipline, Greene understood the importance of providing for his men and never hesitated to agitate on their behalf. Indeed, on October 10 Greene wrote directly to the president of Congress, John Hancock, demanding more medicines and assistance for sick and wounded soldiers, who he said "exhibit a Spectacle shocking to human feelings, and as the knowledge of their distress spreads through the Country will prove an unsurmountable obstacle to the Recruiting the new Army."

Greene also prudently prepared for the probability of yet another withdrawal, this time inland across New Jersey in the direction of Philadelphia. Exhibiting yet another of his important leadership traits, Greene gave great attention to the details and preparation. He not only established supply depots along the probable route of march for the army across New Jersey, including Princeton and Trenton, but he personally reconnoitered the area involved, inspecting bridges and ascertaining the availability of provisions.

Washington and the main army were soon on the move again, thanks to another belated effort by Howe to outflank the Americans. On October 12, 4,000 British soldiers clambered aboard transports at Kip's Bay and moved up the East River. Passing through Hell's Gate, they landed at Throg's Neck in what is now the Bronx. This move made good strategic sense, for it placed Howe's forces to the north and east of Washington's position. If his men could move inland quickly, they could trap Washington on Manhattan and destroy him.

Unfortunately for Howe, he selected a poor location for his landing. Throg's Neck was almost an island, with only one road moving inland, surrounded on both sides by marsh. A small number of Pennsylvania riflemen under Colonel Edward Hand held the bridge and were able to hold the British at bay until reinforcements could come. Over the following six days, Howe embarked his men and moved farther north into Long Island Sound, landing at Pell's Point.

On the road north of Pell's Point at Eastchester, Colonel John Glover and a brigade of 750 Americans sought to block the 4,000 British troops. Not surprisingly, Glover was forced to withdraw, but his men inflicted more casualties on the British than they themselves sustained, and, six days later and a half dozen miles farther north at Mamaroneck, the Delaware regiment attacked and defeated a force of some 500 Loyalists.

Washington had already concluded that he could not remain in Manhattan, and he withdrew north, paralleling the British move to the east. Both armies headed for White Plains. Washington, however, left behind Colonel Robert Magaw and some 2,000 men at Fort Washington in the hopes that Magaw in this position and Greene with 3,500 men at Fort Lee across the river might be able to block any British move up the Hudson.

Washington and the rest of the army, some 14,000 men in all, arrived at White Plains on October 22. Howe delayed at New Rochelle long enough to enable Washington to establish a defensive position, but when 5,000 Hessians under Lieutenant General Wilhelm von Knyphausen arrived, Howe left half of them at New Rochelle and set out with the remainder and his own troops toward White Plains. With about 14,000 men, his own force was comparable in size to that of Washington.

In the Battle of White Plains on October 28, the Continental Army fought well, but the militia again broke and ran, uncovering the American right flank and leaving Washington no option but to withdraw. Losses are variously reported but probably amounted to several hundred killed and wounded on each side, and the British also took several hundred Americans prisoner.

Washington now withdrew northward. Howe, reinforced to 20,000 men, did not pursue, but rather turned west to Dobbs Ferry on the Hudson before moving south to envelop Magaw's force at Fort Washington. Washington left Charles Lee and 6,000 men at Castle Hill to block the British from moving north, then withdrew with the rest of his army northwest to Peekskill, where he crossed over the Hudson to Haverstraw on November 10, then marched south to Hackensack, New Jersey, several miles west of Fort Lee.

Washington had committed a major military error, dividing his already inferior forces and leaving Magaw at Fort Washington where the garrison there might easily be cut off. Greene and other officers supported Washington's decision, believing that if the British tried to take the entrenchments more than two hundred feet above the river, they would suffer the same fate as at Breed's Hill; but at Fort Washington, if British ships were in the Hudson, it would not be possible to withdraw as had been the case with Charlestown Neck at Boston. Greene made several inspection trips across the Hudson to the fort and even increased its garrison by sending over another regiment, until the defenders numbered nearly 3,000 men.

On November 5, despite being fired on from Fort Washington, three British ships managed to get past the fort and make their way north up the Hudson. Learning of this, Washington wrote Greene on November 8, "If we cannot prevent Vessels passing up, and the Enemy are possessed of the surrounding Country, what valuable purpose can it answer to attempt to hold a post from which the expected Benefit cannot be had." Washington told Greene that he did not think it wise to "hazard the Men and Stores at Mount [Fort] Washington, but as you are on the Spot, leave it to you to give such Orders as to evacuating Mount Washington as you judge best, and so far revoking the Order given Colo Magaw to defend it to the last."

Greene did not intend to yield Fort Washington to the British, especially after Magaw told him that, if besieged, he could hold out until December. Certainly Greene erred when he reported to Washington the next day, "Upon the whole I cannot help thinking the Garrison is of advantage, and I cannot conceive the garrison to be in any great danger. The men can be brought off at any time."

On November 15, however, Howe sent 10,000 men against Fort Washington. That day a British officer appeared under a flag of truce to demand the fort's surrender. Magaw refused, saying that the defenders would fight to the last man. Greene crossed the Hudson to confer with Magaw and then returned to New Jersey late that night. The next morning, Washington as well as Generals Greene, Israel Putnam, and Hugh Mercer, and two other officers, were preparing to cross again when they heard cannon fire marking the beginning of the British land assault. The generals crossed to the New York side only to find British troops advancing on Fort Washington from three directions. Greene urged Washington to depart, offering to remain in command of the fort. Putnam and Mercer followed suit. Washington agreed to leave but also insisted the other three generals accompany him. The four were then rowed back across the river.

Supported by fire from ships in the Hudson, Howe's forces stormed Fort Washington several hours later. In this battle the British actually suffered more killed and wounded than did the defenders. While British losses amounted to 78 killed and 374 wounded, 59 Americans died, and another 96 were wounded. But American losses in men taken prisoner and in supplies were staggering. At Fort Washington, the British captured 230 officers and 2,607 soldiers. They also secured 146 cannon, 2,800 muskets, 12,000 shot and shell, and 400,000 musket cartridges. This battle ranks with the surrender of Charleston in 1780 as one of the two worst Patriot defeats of the entire war.

To a considerable extent, the debacle was Greene's fault. Certainly it was his worst military judgment of the war. It is also true, however, that Washington had arrived in the vicinity in time to order an evacuation. In a report to Congress on November 16, Washington accepted responsibility, but he also did not hesitate to blame Greene:

> I determined agreeable to the Advice of the most of the General Officers, to risque something to defend the Post on the East Side call'd Mount Washington. . . . Reflecting upon the smallness of the Garrison and the Difficulty of their holding it, if Genl. Howe should fall upon it with his whole Force, I wrote to Genl. Greene who had the Command on the Jersey Shore, directing him to govern himself by Circumstances, and to retain or evacuate the Post as he should think best. . . . Genl. Greene struck with the Importance of the Post, and the Discouragement which our Evacuation of Posts must necessarily have given, reinforced Colo McGaw with Detachments . . . so as to make up the Number about 2000.

Greene's decision caused a number of influential figures in the army, including General Lee and Washington's aide Joseph Reed, to turn against Greene. Lee even chided Washington, writing to inquire of the commander in chief why he would be "overpersuaded by men of inferior judgment to your own?" It was a difficult time for Greene, for clearly Washington could easily have sacked him for the loss. Greene must have felt very much alone. He wrote Knox on November 17 that he was in "a melancholy temper." He told his friend, "I feel mad, vext, sick and sorry. Never did I need the consoling voice of a friend more than now. Happy should I be to see you." Always concerned about his own military reputation, Greene wanted to know what others were saying: "Pray what is said upon the Occasion. A line from you will be very acceptable."

Despite what Washington had written to Congress, he neither fired Greene nor chose to make him a scapegoat. Perhaps Washington remembered his own difficult learning process in the French and Indian War, and no doubt he knew in his heart that the responsibility for the loss was shared. He also recognized Greene's undoubted leadership abilities and organizational skills. Military knowledge would come with time and experience. A chastened and grateful Greene repaid his commander's confidence with unswerving loyalty. Throughout the war, he remained the commander in chief's stalwart defender and champion.

The fate that had befallen Fort Washington almost was repeated at Fort Lee. That place was now useless, and Greene had already initiated the movement of its 3,000 men and considerable quantities of supplies and ammunition to the interior. Nonetheless, Greene failed to act with urgency. That changed on the morning of November 20, when Greene was awakened with the unwelcome news that the British were fast approaching.

In a bold flanking movement, Major General Charles, Earl Cornwallis led some 4,000 British troops across the Hudson at Closter, six miles above Fort Lee. Although Greene had posted patrols, the British crossed at night and had been able to exploit a gap in the American coverage. The attackers scaled the Palisades on the New Jersey shore and then moved south against Fort Lee. Cornwallis's goal was to get in behind Greene and pin him against the Hudson.

Fortunately for Greene, a colonial farmer raced ahead of the British and alerted him just in time for the bulk of the garrison to escape. Even so, Greene had to abandon some 30 cannon, 300 tents still standing and with the men's blankets, and 1,000 barrels of flour, in addition to other supplies. Greene had already sent off the fort's ammunition. All the garrison escaped, save 8 men killed and 105 who were taken prisoner, some of them malingerers who had broken into the garrison's liquor supply and who were captured quite drunk.

Marching west, Greene joined Washington at Hackensack later that same day. The New York campaign had been an unrelieved disaster. In all, the British had taken at Fort Washington, Fort Lee, and their dependencies, 146 cannon, 12,000 shot and shell, 2,800 muskets, and 400,000 musket cartridges, not to mention tents and other equipment. More than 4,000 men had been lost.

The dispirited Continentals trudged west with the British in dilatory pursuit. On November 22, the Continentals arrived at Newark; and on December 2, they reached Trenton and the Delaware River. Washington called up the New Jersey militia, but few responded. Thomas Paine moved with the army across New Jersey. He had joined Greene's staff as a civilian aide some weeks before, and at night he wrote in camp, no doubt following conversations with Greene and others. From this came his brilliant pamphlet, *The Crisis*. Paine wrote: "These are the times that try men's souls. The summer soldier and the sunshine patriot will, in this crisis, shrink from the service of his country; but he that stands it NOW deserves the love and thanks of man and woman. Tyranny, like Hell, is not easily conquered. Yet we have this consolation with us that the harder the conflict, the more glorious the triumph."

Lee now greatly compounded Washington's problems. Disregarding Washington's orders, he was slow to cross the Hudson. Washington begged Lee to join him swiftly, but Lee proceeded to campaign on his own. Not until December 2–4 did he cross the river to New Jersey, and then he decided to act independently against British outposts in that state, confident he could clear it of British troops. Directly disobeying Washington's orders to join him on the Delaware, Lee remained in Morristown, New Jersey, with his forces. On December 16, a British scouting force under Coronet Banastre Tarleton, with whom Greene would become well acquainted later in the war, captured Lee at his tavern headquarters in Basking Ridge. The Lee bubble quickly burst. When he was released in 1778 there was no longer any talk about Lee possibly replacing Washington. By then the Continental Army had outgrown him.

On December 9, Washington withdrew what remained of his army across the Delaware into Pennsylvania. Both sides then went into winter quarters. Although Howe had pursued Washington into the interior, he had failed to bag his foe. Whether it was Howe's innate caution, the experience of Breed's/Bunker Hill, his assignment as commissioner to negotiate peace, the fact that much of his army consisted of pressed men or mercenaries, the diversion of his mistress, or a combination thereof, Washington had gotten away. But most dispassionate observers probably believed that the war was about over. Come spring and the resumption of campaigning, the British would finish off the rebels. Howe now set up a string of strong outposts along the east bank of the Delaware River at Trenton, Princeton, and other places.

Greene remained optimistic, or tried to be when writing Caty. He told her: "Fortune seems to frown upon the cause of freedom a combination of evils are pressing in upon us on all sides. However, I hope this is the dark part of the night, which generally is just before day."

Washington's force was now down to only about 6,000 men, many of them militia. A large number were sick. The enlistments of most of the regulars would be up on January 1. Washington wrote to his cousin Lund Washington on December 18 that, unless the army were immediately replenished, "I think the game will be pretty well up."

On December 21, Greene wrote to president of the Continental Congress John Hancock. He told Hancock that although he believed the situation to be "critical," it was not yet "desperate." What was required was to regularize army recruitment, establish the artillery, quiet the disaffected, put the currency on a sound footing, and establish an effective supply system and magazines. To accomplish this, it was absolutely necessary that Congress and the states give Washington extraordinary powers, greater than heretofore, "to promote the Establishment of the New Army." Greene assured Hancock, "the General will not exceed his Powers altho' he may sacrifice the Cause." Although it is doubtful that Greene's letter was a deciding factor, a week later Congress passed a resolution giving Washington near dictatorial powers for six months. These powers included the right to appoint officers below the rank of brigadier general.

It was in these dire circumstances at the end of 1776 that Washington risked everything in a desperate gamble. He explained his plan to Greene and the other generals in a meeting in his headquarters on Christmas Eve. The Americans would attack the Hessian outpost at Trenton early on December 26, hoping to catch the German soldiers there off guard following Christmas Day celebrating. Bitter cold, snow, and ice in the river would render the crossing difficult, but the Americans hoped these conditions would also add to the element of surprise. The countersign of "Victory or Death" well describes the operation's nature.

Washington planned three separate crossings of the river. He would accompany the main force of 2,400 men and Knox's 18 pieces of artillery. The crossing occurred on Christmas night in terrible conditions in the middle of a snowstorm. Only Washington's main force attacked, falling on the 1,500 Hessians at Trenton early on the morning of December 26. Greene had perhaps the most difficult assignment of the battle and played an important role. Washington's force came in against Trenton from the northwest in two columns, one under Greene and the other under Sullivan. Greene, accompanied by Washington, had charge of the left wing, which moved against the Hessians from the north. Sullivan led the right wing around the town to block escape from the south.

Never mind that the crossing had taken much longer than anticipated, that the other two of Washington's columns turned back and did not get into the battle at all, or that Colonel Johann Gottlieb Rall, the Hessian commander who was contemptuous of the "rabble" on the other side of the river, had taken few precautions to guard against surprise attack. The colonials won a glorious victory at little cost. Whereas 4 Americans were killed and 8 wounded, Hessian losses were 22 killed and 92 wounded. Rall was mortally wounded. While some 500 Hessians escaped, the Americans took 948 prisoners, including 32 officers. They also captured

6 field pieces and 1,000 muskets and rifles. Washington was determined not to risk his great accomplishment, and his army quickly recrossed the Delaware.

Despite the victory, Washington struggled to hold the army together. Most of his men believed they had done enough and were determined to head home. Let others take up the cause, they said. Armed with a hasty reenlistment bounty of $10 (nearly twice the soldiers' monthly pay of $6), passed by Congress just days before, Washington spoke directly to the affected regiments and appealed to the men in them as equals, telling them that while they had done everything asked of them and more, their country still had great need of them. While this appeal failed to prevent 2,500 men from departing on January 1, 3,000 agreed to stay on.

That same day, Cornwallis arrived at Princeton. Howe was scheduled to return to England to attend to an ailing wife, but following the debacle of Trenton, he canceled his leave and gave Cornwallis 8,000 men to crush the Americans. Correctly convinced that the Americans were about to mount another crossing, Cornwallis detailed three regiments, some 1,200 men, under Lieutenant Colonel Charles Mawhood, to hold Princeton and about as many men at Maidenhead (now Lawrenceville), while he left with the remaining 5,500 to seek out his adversary.

On December 30, Washington crossed the Delaware for a third time, establishing his command center at Trenton. In this operation, Greene commanded a division of some 1,400 men in four brigades, all of which were under strength. Accustomed to the slow, deliberate movements of Howe, Washington was surprised to learn of Cornwallis's rapid approach on January 1. Greene immediately pushed skirmishers forward in an effort to try to delay the British approach until dark.

Counting militia, Washington now had about 5,000 men deployed south of Trenton along Assunpink Creek. Cornwallis appeared to have the Americans trapped with their backs against the Delaware. With his men tired and hungry from their long march, and confident of victory the next day, Cornwallis ignored advice from some of his officers that he press forward that evening. He assured his staff that he would "bag the old fox" (Washington) in the morning.

On the night of January 1–2, Washington carried out a risky maneuver. He left a few men behind to fuel campfires and to work on entrenchments with shovels at certain points where the British were bound to hear them. He then had all the rest strike camp, cross the creek, and move around the British left flank. The remaining men followed at daybreak.

Advancing along the little-used Quaker Road to Princeton, Washington personally rallied his men when the American advance fell back during an attack by two of Mawhood's regiments marching to join Cornwallis. The Continentals then routed the British. Washington's force suffered only 35 casualties, although one of these was Brigadier General Hugh Mercer, who was killed. Washington claimed British casualties totaling some 100 dead and 399 wounded or captured, but Howe reported 28 dead, 58 wounded, and 187 missing. The Americans captured two British guns but were unable to remove them for want of horses. Before Cornwallis could arrive with his own troops, Washington moved on to the hilly terrain in the vicinity of Morristown, which Greene had secured earlier when he was at Fort Lee, and where the army now went into winter quarters.

In the span of only ten days, Washington had restored confidence in the revolutionary cause. The small victories of Trenton and Princeton are rightly regarded as critical battles, perhaps the most critical, of the war. The effect on the American people was instantaneous and dramatic. In place of despair, there was now confidence that the Americans could indeed ultimately triumph. The victories also served to bolster the confidence of the army in Washington's leadership, so badly shaken by the New York debacle. Howe now recalled Cornwallis to New York. An aggressive move by Howe in the winter might indeed have ended the war, but Howe's own prudence was reinforced by the setbacks of Trenton and Princeton, and he was also enjoying being feted by Tories in New York City.

Washington now relied on Greene completely. When Washington's adjutant Joseph Reed left the army, Greene took his place for several weeks and the two men grew even closer. Greene could not have been more pleased. He wrote Caty on January 20, 1777, "I am exceeding happy in the full confidence of his Excellency General Washington, and I found [that confidence] to increase every hour, the more [difficult] and distressing our affairs grew."

When Rhode Island leaders had sent an urgent appeal to Washington in December 1776 asking that Greene be returned to the state to defend it against British attack, Washington refused. Indeed, during the winter of 1776–77, Washington appealed to Congress to promote Greene and two others to the rank of lieutenant general, but Congress refused to advance anyone beyond the rank of major general, save for Washington himself. Still, according to Greene biographer Theodore Thayer, Washington had already decided, were he to be captured or become incapacitated for any reason, that Greene, not Lee, was the best qualified officer to succeed him.

CHAPTER FIVE

THE WAR IN PENNSYLVANIA: BRANDYWINE AND GERMANTOWN

GREENE HAD HOPED FOR A WINTER CAMPAIGN BY THE Continental Army, perhaps against New Brunswick, that would ultimately clear New Jersey of the British. But any hopes of this were dashed by the need to rebuild the army. Most of the men who had agreed to remain in the army for an additional six weeks following the Battle of Trenton now departed—indeed many of them deserted even before that date—and Washington and his officers had to begin anew. Washington was left with only about 3,000 men, but just a third of these were Continental Army soldiers. The majority was militia. Meanwhile, the Americans sent out small forces to attack British foraging parties, utilizing guerrilla tactics.

Again, supply problems abounded, particularly food. Even worse, disease was rampant, including smallpox. Greene suggested to Washington that he take the radical step of having the entire army inoculated. The commander-in-chief agreed, and the smallpox epidemic was soon ended.

Greene spent most of the winter simply trying to secure the welfare of his men. He also kept up his correspondence with John Adams. The two men continued to disagree on general officer promotions. Indeed, Congress's system of limiting major generals to two per state did seem a strange arrangement. Greene, never one to mince words, informed Adams, "I fear your late Promotions will give great disgust to many. . . ."

As a sign of the confidence Washington placed in Greene, in late March 1777 he sent Greene to Philadelphia. Washington explained to Congress that he had selected Greene "[because he] is so much in my confidence, so intimately acquainted with my ideas, with our strength and our weaknesses, with everything regarding the army." Greene's assignment was to try to restore relations between the army and Congress that had become frayed during the winter, but a major task was to impress on Congress the necessity for regular pay for the soldiers, understandably a matter of great concern for the commander in chief.

This was both Greene's first visit to Philadelphia and his initial meeting with many members of Congress. He spent two hours before Congress, pleading Washington's case and answering questions from members regarding military affairs. Greene also met informally on several evenings with Congressmen. He did not come away with a favorable impression, writing Washington on March 25, "There is so much deliberation and waste of time in the execution of business before this assembly that my patience is almost exhausted."

Like most of the republic's military leaders, Greene had little patience with airy and long-winded debates while soldiers went hungry and were ill-clothed and were in want of medicine and military supplies. In May, Greene noted that "Congress have so many of these talking Gentlemen among them that they tire themselves and every body else with their long, laboured speeching that is calculated more to display their own talents than promote the publick interest."

Greene always enjoyed the company of attractive younger women, and he wrote to Caty on his return to Morristown on March 30, reminding her that it had been "eight long months" since he had "tasted the pleasures of domestick felicity." He then went on to inform her that "The young ladies of Philadelphia appear angelick. A few months Separation more will put my virtue to a new tryal. If you dont wish to put my resolution to the torture, bless me with your company; that is, providing your health and other circumstances favors my wishes." One can only imagine the reaction from Caty, who, unknown to Greene, had given birth on March 11 to their second child, a daughter, Martha Washington Greene. Caty was also recovering from a bout of pneumonia, and it would be several more months before she was able to join her husband in camp. Learning of his wife's illness, Greene entreated her to get well and to join him as soon as possible.

Meanwhile, the thoughts of generals on both sides turned to war plans for the spring. Greene expressed surprise that the British were slow to act, but the decisions were actually being made in London by the man charged with running the war, Secretary of State for the American Department Lord George Germain, and communication was slow. Germain ultimately approved two diametrically opposed plans for 1777.

The first of these was a polycentric scheme advanced by Lieutenant General John Burgoyne, the main part of which was an operation to be led by Burgoyne himself from Canada. Burgoyne planned to move down the traditional river-lake invasion route. A secondary feint under Lieutenant Colonel Barry St. Leger would draw off colonial strength to the west. Burgoyne's main force would then meet up in the vicinity of Albany, New York, with forces sent up the Hudson by Howe from New York City. Burgoyne believed that with New England cut off from the rest of the colonies, the revolution would wither on the vine. Of course, Howe might have achieved the same result the previous year after driving Washington from New York, but had chosen to chase his prey across New Jersey instead.

At the same time Germain approved Burgoyne's plan, he also gave approval to Howe for a move against Philadelphia. This was the move Greene had expected the British to make. Howe reasoned that Washington would have to fight to defend the capital, and once he had been soundly defeated and Philadelphia captured, the revolution would be pretty much at an end. Howe kept Carleton, the British commander in Canada, fully informed of his plans, telling him that he would leave a corps in New York, elements of which he hoped might act in support of Burgoyne's plans, but that he would have the bulk of the army occupied in the Philadelphia campaign.

Although some have gone so far as accusing Howe of setting up Burgoyne to fail, this probably was not the case. Howe no doubt assumed, correctly, that he would be assisting Burgoyne in drawing off sizeable numbers of Continental Army troops who otherwise might have been sent north. Regardless, the British campaign of 1777 was riddled with poor planning, lack of coordination, and overconfidence on the part of the two chief British field commanders, especially Burgoyne. Aware that Howe was not doing as he wished, he proceeded anyway. The chief fault, however, lay with the inept Germain, who approved two basically contrary plans.

Meanwhile, Washington believed he had little choice but to stand on the defensive. Continental Army troop numbers had improved somewhat during the winter, so that by spring Washington had somewhat more than 7,000 men under arms. His enemy was still far more numerous, however. The British retained two posts in New Jersey, New Brunswick and Perth Amboy, and Washington had Greene draw up plans for an attack on New Brunswick. But in a council of war held on May 2, Greene joined all the other generals in voting against it. The consensus was that the army was incapable of mounting an effective attack against a well-fortified position.

In mid-May, well aware of probable British plans to invade from Canada, Washington dispatched both Greene and Knox to examine defensive positions on the Hudson south of West Point in hopes of controlling that key waterway. The two generals and several other officers rode to Peekskill, New York, then traveled along the river. Pronouncing the defenses inadequate, they soon returned to Morristown.

The next month, June, Caty finally was able to join her husband in Morristown. Their two children remained behind in Rhode Island with Greene's brothers. Caty's arrival coincided with a serious row between the army and Congress. It was to bring to an end Greene's friendship with John Adams and almost cost him his military career.

A number of foreign officers had arrived to join the American cause, many of them signed on by Silas Deane, one of the American commissioners in France authorized by Congress to recruit military specialists. While many of these officers proved quite capable, others were certainly not. Greene was among those incensed that foreigners of dubious distinction were being given positions of leadership over deserving American officers. Washington was of like mind, but he let the outspoken Greene lead the fight.

Matters came to a head over Deane's enlistment of French army general Philip Charles Trouson Du Coudray as chief of the Continental Army artillery, thus replacing Greene's ally and friend Henry Knox. Du Coudray arrived in America in May 1777, met with Washington at Morristown, and then proceeded to Philadelphia to present his credentials to Congress. His extensive entourage reportedly included eighteen officers and ten sergeants.

Knox, Sullivan, and Greene were all outraged at Du Coudray's appointment. On May 28, 1777, Greene wrote to Adams in protest: "The impropriety of putting a foraigner at the head of such a Department must be obvious to every body. Besides the impropriety, you will deprive the Army of a most valuable Officer. . . ." In this, Greene of course meant Knox. Adams agreed and replied that he shared Greene's concern over the "Danger of entrusting so many important Commands to foreigners." Deane had certainly "exceeded his Powers," and Adams assured Greene that he himself opposed the appointment and was certain that Du Coudray would find "few advocates" in Congress.

Greene was also incensed to discover that Du Coudray's commission in the Continental Army dated from August 1, 1776, making him senior to Greene by eight days. Ignoring Adams's sympathetic response, and apparently without first consulting Washington, Greene now took the most ill-considered action of his military career. On July 1, he wrote to John Hancock, president of the Continental Congress:

> A report is circulating here at Camp that Monsieur du Coudray a French Gentleman is appointed a Major General in the service of the United States, his rank to commence from the first of last

> August. If the report be true it will lay me under the necessity of resigning my Commission as his appointment supercedes me in command. I beg youl acquaint me with respect to the truth of the report, and if true inclose me a permit to retire.

Knox and Sullivan also wrote letters of their own threatening similar action. Members of Congress were not pleased with what they regarded as blatant military interference in an area they considered their own prerogative, especially as they had not yet approved Du Coudray's appointment. On July 7, 1777, Congress passed a resolution instructing Washington to convey its displeasure to the three generals and inform them that it considered their letters "an attempt to influence their Decisions, an invasion of the liberties of the people, and indicating a want of confidence in the justice of Congress." The resolution went on to demand that the three generals "make proper acknowledgments of an interference of so dangerous a tendency," and it concluded with an invitation to the three to make good on their threat: "But if any of those officers are unwilling to serve their country, under the authority of Congress, they shall be at liberty to resign their commissions and retire." At the same time, however, Congress also chided Deane for entering into agreements that superseded American officers.

That same day, July 7, Adams wrote Greene a long letter noting the resolution and chastising him for his conduct. Misspelling his name, Adams reminded "my Friend General Green" of his own misgivings and those of members of Congress about the Du Coudray appointment and telling him that he should have written a private letter instead of a public one threatening resignation. Greene, Sullivan, and Knox, he said, had been guilty of "Rashness, Passion and even Wantonness in this Proceeding." Adams urged Greene to apologize and declare publicly that he had "the fullest

Confidence in the Justice of Congress and their Deliberations for the public Good." If he could not do this in "truth and Sincerity," then Greene "ought to leave the service." Greene apparently never replied. His friendship with Adams now ended. Although Adams wrote to Greene in March 1780 from Paris, it was months before the letter arrived, Greene did not respond until January 1782, and there is no evidence that Adams ever received it.

Greene neither apologized nor resigned, but he also never again attempted to influence Congress in such a manner. On August 11, 1777, Congress decided to make Du Coudray "Inspector general of ordnance and military manufactories." But just two months later the Frenchman drowned while attempting to ride his horse onto the Schuylkill Ferry.

The Du Coudray affair was soon subsumed by the return of the war. Learning that Howe had pulled his garrison out of Perth Amboy, Greene expected an immediate move overland against Philadelphia. This did not occur, however. To the north, meanwhile, Burgoyne's army was in motion. St. Leger's small diversionary force of British regulars and Indian allies was contained by militia and Continental troops at Oriskany, but Burgoyne's main body pushed steadily southward.

Smaller Continental Army and militia forces, which were under the Northern Army commander, aristocratic New York Major General Philip Schuyler, retreated, destroying what might be useful to the British. Fort Ticonderoga fell rather easily to Burgoyne on June 6, 1777. Schuyler called on Washington to send Greene north, but the commander in chief refused, sending instead Major Generals Benjamin Lincoln and Benedict Arnold. Schuyler's policy (withdrawing before superior strength and forcing the British to dissipate their own resources to defend a long communication line back to Canada) was the correct one in the circumstances, but it also set off a great deal of criticism, which ambitious Major General Horatio Gates used to his advantage. Gates blamed Ticonderoga's fall on Schuyler and helped engineer both the latter's recall and his own appointment to succeed him.

Endeavoring to send north what reinforcements he could spare, Washington was also forced to deal with an entirely new military front, for on July 23 Howe sailed from New York with 13,000 troops in some 260 ships. Washington could not discount the possibility of a feint and a British return to New York and move up the Hudson. The Continental Army thus spent considerable time marching and countermarching, but in early August Washington became convinced that Philadelphia was Howe's objective, and he began to move the army in that direction. When the British fleet sailed into Chesapeake Bay, it confirmed Washington's assumption. Greene understood the importance of fighting for Philadelphia, but he also believed that, as a military objective, the capital paled next to the Hudson, and that Howe's ultimate design was New England. Philadelphia was "the American Diana; she must be preserved at all events . . . but in my opinion [it] is an object of far less importance than the North [Hudson] River."

Washington now moved the bulk of his forces south to meet Howe. On August 24, 1777, his army of 11,000 men, including Greene and his division, marched through Philadelphia. Howe began disembarking his men at Head of Elk (Elkton, Maryland) the next day. As Howe well knew, defending Philadelphia, the seat of Congress and a large city, was a challenge Washington could hardly refuse. He expected to force Washington into a set-piece battle and, this time, to destroy him.

On August 26, Washington, Greene, and French aristocrat and now Continental Army Major General Marie Joseph du Motier, Marquis de Lafayette, accompanied only by a cavalry guard, set off on a rather foolhardy reconnaissance in unfamiliar territory and watched the British forces come ashore. That night a sudden storm came up, and the generals spent the night in an empty farmhouse, which turned out to belong to a Tory. Fortunately, no one gave the alarm, and the next day the party returned to the main American lines at Wilmington.

On August 31, Greene wrote to his brother Jacob that he hoped Howe would give the Continentals "a little time to collect," and that they did not care "how soon he begins the frolick." Greene expressed "the greatest hopes if Providence dont think proper to punnish us further with the calamities of war to give General How a deadly wound."

As it worked out, Washington had ample time to move forces into defensive positions south of the capital. By September 1, thanks to reinforcements and new recruits, he had in place some 16,000 men between Wilmington and Philadelphia, but 3,000 of these were unreliable militia. Greene's division was camped at White Clay Creek, six miles to the southeast of Wilmington, but Greene, as was his wont, spent much of the first week of September in the saddle, scouting the countryside and familiarizing himself with the terrain.

Washington remained optimistic, regarding the coming battle as an opportunity. He detached small forces, both to harass the British and to provide information on their movements, while at the same time establishing a defensive position with the main army. Skirmishes occurred at Elkton on August 28, at Wilmington, Delaware, on August 31, and at Cooch's Bridge, Delaware, on September 3.

Washington was undecided on where to take up his main defensive position. On August 28, he moved Greene's and Stephen's divisions to White Clay Creek. Then, following a council of war, on September 6 the army relocated to the north side of Red Clay Creek near Newport, astride the main road to Philadelphia. Learning that the British had divested themselves of most of their equipment and were preparing to move, Washington ordered his own baggage and tents sent north of Brandywine Creek.

Before dawn on the morning of September 8, the British began their advance, but not toward Washington's position. Sending only a detachment toward Red Clay Creek, Howe set most of this army in motion northward toward Philadelphia. Washington believed this to be an effort to flank his own position, and he hastily withdrew well before dawn on September 9 to Chadd's Ford on the Brandywine, across the more northerly Philadelphia Road.

"Creek" was an incorrect term for the Brandywine, a tributary of the Delaware, for it could be crossed easily only at several widely placed fords. Greene, who had favored the Chadd's Ford position earlier, pointed out that it would give the Continentals the high ground and force the British to attack uphill. Pennsylvania officers informed Washington that there were no other fords for a dozen miles north of those covered by his troops. Washington trusted this information, and he neither reconnoitered himself nor sent a trustworthy subordinate to do so. This carelessness nearly proved fatal, for the information was incorrect, and British scouts soon located undefended fords.

Howe's forces arrived in the vicinity of Chadd's Ford early on the morning of September 10. Assisted by area Loyalists, Howe and his two corps commanders, Cornwallis and Knyphausen, personally explored the area and thus were far better informed of circumstances than was Washington. With a good knowledge of American dispositions, Howe decided to employ the tactics that had worked well for him in the Battle of Long Island: a frontal diversion and a wide envelopment as the principal British effort. Knyphausen with a mixed British and Hessian force of 5,000 men was to make the frontal diversion to fix Washington in place, while Cornwallis led 8,000 British troops in the wide envelopment around the American right in hopes of getting in behind Washington and bagging his entire army.

Washington, meanwhile, made his own troop dispositions. He placed Greene's division, considered his best troops, in the center left of the Patriot line at Chadd's Ford. With the water there only knee deep, this ford was the logical place for the British to attempt to cross. To Greene's immediate left, Major General John Armstrong and his Pennsylvania militia covered Pyle's Ford. Steep ground worked against a British crossing there, however. Sullivan commanded the American right, with Major Generals William Alexander, Lord Stirling, and Adam Stephen's divisions stretched out along Brandywine Creek and covering both Brinton's and Painter's Fords. A small detachment under Colonel Moses Hazen guarded the far American right at Wister's Ford about four miles from Chadd's Ford.

The battle occurred on September 11. That morning Knyphausen's men tested the Continental Army defenders at Chadd's Ford and then withdrew. Greene and the others expected a massive assault by Howe's entire army, but already at 4 a.m. Cornwallis and Howe had set out on a broad arc with the flanking force about fifteen miles from Chadd's Ford and several miles beyond the extreme American right under Hazen, crossing the Brandywine at unguarded Jeffrie's Ford. Washington now received conflicting reports. News of the flanking attack almost led him to issue an order for an attack against the badly outnumbered Knyphausen, and Greene rode back from a meeting with Washington to prepare for such, but Washington changed his mind when he received a report that led him to believe that Knyphausen's movement might be a feint. Washington refused to proceed until he had confirmation of British dispositions.

Early that afternoon Washington received definitive word that the bulk of the British forces were indeed across the Brandywine and were preparing to roll up the American right. True to form, however, Howe delayed for a time, probably missing the chance to destroy Washington's army. This delay gave Sullivan time to rotate his force 90 degrees, refusing his flank to meet the British attack beginning at 4 p.m. At the same time, Washington ordered Greene to remain in place in the event of a move by Knyphausen supporting Howe.

Sullivan's men, vastly outnumbered by the attacking British, soon gave way. Indeed, most retreated in panic. In these circumstances, Washington decided he had no choice but to order Greene to march to buttress Sullivan and hold the road to Philadelphia. Defense of the ford would be left to the artillery of Brigadier General Anthony Wayne, Brigadier General William Maxwell, and Colonel Thomas Proctor.

Greene immediately swung into action, his men covering four miles under a hot sun in only forty-five minutes. His troops included Colonel George Weedon's steady Virginia regiment and Brigadier General Peter Mühlenberg's regiment. There was no time to try to reorganize Sullivan's force; instead, on their arrival Greene's men simply fixed bayonets, opened their ranks to let Sullivan's men pass through, and then closed again to meet the onrushing British. Knox's artillery provided effective enfilading fire. Mühlenberg in particular steadied the Americans, riding among them on horseback to encourage them in what became a battle at close quarters with the bayonet, in which the Americans were outnumbered two to one.

Although retrieving the situation was beyond Greene's means, he and his men were able to hold the British long enough for the arrival of darkness. Slowly Greene fell back, his men firing in volleys as they withdrew. At the same time, hearing the heavy sounds of the engagement, Knyphausen launched an attack of his own, supported by artillery, against the now-weakened American center. It, too, soon gave way. Nightfall saved the army, permitting Washington and the bulk of his forces to make a more or less orderly withdrawal toward Chester.

American casualties in the Battle of the Brandywine were more than twice those of the British: 200 killed, 700–800 wounded, and almost 400 prisoners, as against 99 killed, 488 wounded, and 6 missing for the British. American morale, however, remained high, and the army had escaped to fight another day. Greene had played a key role. Optimistic, he reported to Caty, "You may expect to hear of another Action in a few days. Our troops are in good health and high Spirits and wish for action again. I have full confidence the Lord of Hosts will give us Victory."

After the battle, the prideful Greene, ever conscious of his military reputation, inquired of Washington why the commander in chief's dispatches had not mentioned him or singled out Weedon for special praise. Washington calmed Greene with flattery, reportedly telling him: "You, sir, are considered my favorite officer. Weedon's brigade, like myself, are Virginians; should I applaud them for their achievement under your command, I should be charged with partiality; jealousy will be excited, and the service injured." Greene accepted the explanation.

The natural consequence of Brandywine Creek was the British occupation of Philadelphia. Following marching and countermarching and the threat of yet another major engagement, Howe entered the half-deserted city on September 26. Three thousand British troops occupied Philadelphia; the remaining 9,000 established camp outside it, most of them at Germantown, five miles to the north. Meanwhile, Admiral Richard Howe set about destroying the American naval forces on the Delaware that had obliged his brother to approach the city by way of the Chesapeake.

Howe's seizure of Philadelphia was a hollow victory, for it did not bring him the masses of Loyalists for which he had hoped. Also, Burgoyne was about to lose an entire British Army in northern New York. When Benjamin Franklin, who was in Paris, was informed that Howe had taken Philadelphia, he is said to have remarked that it would be more proper to say that "Philadelphia has captured General Howe."

Following the British occupation of Philadelphia, Washington, reinforced to about 11,000 men, decided to attempt a surprise descent on Howe's main encampment at Germantown. Howe had foolishly discounted the possibility of an American attack and had not even entrenched his forces there. On September 28, Washington summoned his generals to a council of war at Pennypacker's Mills, Pennsylvania. Earlier that same day, word had arrived at Washington's headquarters of a major engagement to the north between British and American forces at Saratoga, with reports of heavy British casualties. On this occasion, however, Greene joined nine other generals of eighteen present in voting against an immediate attack. Instead, the majority urged that the army be moved to within a dozen miles of Germantown and there await reinforcements, which were soon expected. Washington concurred and soon the army was underway.

On October 3, Washington summoned another conference and informed his generals that Howe had weakened his forces by sending a detachment against an American fort on the Delaware. Only 8,500–9,000 British troops now remained at Germantown. With reinforcements following the Battle of Brandywine, Washington would have 11,000 men, although 3,000 of these were militia. This time the generals concurred, voting unanimously in favor of an attack.

As it turned out, Washington's plan was too complicated for his largely untrained forces to execute. It called for four columns to advance independently and for each to attack the British from a different direction. They were to move during the night of October 3–4. Night movements are notoriously difficult to execute, even for a well-trained force, and Washington's army certainly was not such. The precise coordination required was simply beyond the army's abilities.

The Americans left camp at dusk on October 3. There were two flanking columns of militia and two center columns of Continentals. Greene commanded the leftmost Continental corps that would come in from the north, consisting of divisions under Stephen and Brigadier General Alexander McDougall: some 5,000 men, more than half of the Continental Army force. Washington went with the rightmost corps under Sullivan to come in from the northwest. Sullivan had his own division and those of Brigadier Generals Thomas Conway and Anthony Wayne, with Stirling in reserve.

A major problem was that each of the columns would have different distances to travel. Greene's was the longest—about nineteen miles—while the other three each had to march about fifteen miles. Washington's plan called for the three columns to reach their staging areas about 2 a.m., pause there for two hours, and then attack at 4 a.m.

As it turned out, all columns fell behind schedule. The two flanking columns of militia on the extreme left and right never got into the fight. That to Greene's left, some 1,100 Maryland militia under Brigadier General William Smallwood, became confused in the fog. Those on the right, General Armstrong's column of 1,500 Pennsylvania militia, moved south along the Ridge Pike to the Wissahican River, near where it joins the Schuylkill River, but went no further, being content to lob a few artillery shells across the Wissahican into Knyphausen's camp.

This meant that the Continental Army units had to bear the battle alone. Only Sullivan's column was in place by 2 a.m. Greene had farther to move and was handicapped by heavy fog. His guides lost the way, and the men then had to retrace their steps for four miles. Meanwhile, Tories in the area alerted the British to the Patriot movements.

Washington, with Sullivan, assumed that the other columns were in place, but when the battle began at dawn, Sullivan's division and Wayne's brigade had to engage the British alone for about forty-five minutes in heavy fog before Greene's men finally joined the fight. Nonetheless, the Americans drove back a British light infantry battalion along the Skippack Road toward the main British camp.

The British took up positions in and around the two-foot-thick stone walls of the Chew house in central Germantown and other stone dwellings, which proved largely impervious to American small arms and even artillery fire. Wayne's men pressed forward, but Knox convinced Washington when he came up that they needed to take the Chew house rather than leave a fortress position in the American rear. Washington then ordered Maxwell's New Jersey brigade to assault the Chew house position. This held, despite at least seventy Americans killed and many more wounded in the attempt to take it.

Nonetheless, the American advance was still proceeding when, at the critical point in the battle, Greene's men at last arrived. Greene sent forward Stephen's division, but in the morning fog and thick smoke of the battle, this unit, hindered by the fact that its commander was completely drunk, got off course and instead of converging with the remainder of Greene's force, mistook Wayne's men for British soldiers and opened fire on them. Wayne's soldiers, convinced in turn that the troops firing on them were British, returned fire and then, almost out of ammunition, broke and ran back past the Chew house. Carrying other American units along with them, they exposed Conway's left flank and allowed the British to rally.

Meanwhile, Mühlenberg's Virginians employed the bayonet against the British in the town meeting house and took one hundred prisoners, but they had advanced too far and were then cut off. With all their officers wounded and completely surrounded, the regiment was forced to surrender. Cornwallis then arrived with reinforcements who had double-timed from Philadelphia, while Washington, Sullivan, and Wayne rallied their men. Greene, unaware of what had transpired, continued his advance, but was now alone. When he became aware of events, he placed his men so as to cover the other American units, recklessly exposing himself to British fire as he rallied his men.

At about 9 a.m. the British launched a successful counterattack, and Greene had no choice but to fall back. Howe pursued the Americans about five miles back up the Germantown Pike, but the British pursuit ground to a halt at sunset thanks to poor roads and the actions of Greene's infantry, Wayne's artillery, and a cavalry detachment under the Polish Count Casimir Pulaski. The Americans then returned to their own camp.

The battle had lasted some three hours. American losses included 152 killed, 521 wounded, and about 400 taken prisoner. British losses were half those of the Americans: 71 killed, 450 wounded, and 14 missing. Although the militia had again performed poorly, Washington could at least be pleased that the Continentals had fought well until they had been fired on by their own men. The Americans also had brought off all of their guns.

Following the battle, Washington promptly cashiered Stephen and gave his division to Lafayette. Although Greene came in for some criticism for his delay in reaching the battlefield, Washington did not think him at fault. After the war, Greene wrote Colonel Henry Lee: "At Germaintown, I was evidently degraced, altho I think if ever I merited any thing it was for my exertions on that day."

Meanwhile, in northern New York, the Americans were winning victories. Burgoyne had continued his advance, despite knowing by early August that Howe was not coming to reinforce him, that St. Leger's diversionary attack had failed, and that his long supply lines to Canada were under attack from partisans and would be rendered untenable by the onset of winter. On August 16, 1777, the Continentals won an important victory at Bennington, Vermont, when they cut off a foraging force of Hessians and forced them to surrender. The British suffered 207 killed and 700 captured against American casualties of only 30 killed and wounded. The Continentals also secured much needed supplies and weapons.

Then, near Saratoga, New York, Burgoyne's advance ground to a halt, and the Americans triumphed at Freeman's Farm (First Saratoga) on September 19, and at Bemis Heights (Second Saratoga) on October 7, only three days after Germantown. As a consequence of these battles, known collectively as the Battle of Saratoga, Burgoyne surrendered his entire army of some 5,500 men. The British were also obliged to yield Ticonderoga and the Hudson Highlands. Howe had won several battles and taken the capital of Philadelphia, but the city was devoid of military significance. The French government understood this; after word of Saratoga, it reversed its policy of extending only secret aid, and, on February 6, 1778, entered into a formal treaty of alliance with the United States. On March 11, Great Britain and France were at war. This French intervention was crucial and marked the turning point in the war.

Meanwhile, the British had opened operations against American Forts Mifflin and Mercer that controlled access via the Delaware River to Philadelphia. Some vessels of the Pennsylvania Navy as well as hulks and cheveaux-de-frise (large weighted, sunken wooden boxes with long iron spikes) also barred their way, but the two forts were the chief barriers. The British were then short of supplies, and transports with munitions, clothing, and foodstuffs were in the river waiting to proceed upstream.

Mifflin, named for the army quartermaster general, was situated on Mud Island near the mouth of the Schuylkill River in the river itself. Mercer, named for the general killed in the Battle of Princeton, was somewhat farther up the river on the New Jersey shore. Greene's cousin, Christopher Greene, commanded the garrison of 400 Rhode Islanders at Fort Mercer.

On October 22, Hessian troops attacked Mercer without

preliminary bombardment. The defenders exacted a heavy toll, mortally wounding the Hessian commander and driving off the assault. The Hessians suffered 371 casualties; the Americans lost but 37. Greene was delighted that his fellow Rhode Islanders had acquitted themselves so well.

At Fort Mifflin, the British set up batteries and in late October commenced siege operations, beginning a protracted bombardment. The defenders conducted a gallant defense, endeavoring to repair damage to the fort at night, but the garrison was slowly being reduced. In early November, Washington moved the army closer to Philadelphia, hoping to draw off Howe from the siege, but this did not have the intended result. With Mifflin under increasing pressure, Washington agreed to the pleas of its commander and authorized a withdrawal, which occurred on November 15.

With Fort Mifflin now in British hands, Washington sent Greene across the Delaware with some 3,000 men to reinforce Fort Mercer. However, Cornwallis also crossed the river on November 18 with 2,000 men. Determined to end American resistance, he reached Mercer first. Concluding that the fort was lost, Christopher Greene torched the fort and all supplies the men could not carry away. The garrison then made good its escape. Greene learned of the loss while moving through Burlington, New Jersey.

Greene was nonetheless eager to take on Cornwallis. He wrote Washington on November 21, "If it is possible to make an attack upon 'em with a prospect of success it shall be done." Washington sent his approval the next day.

As it worked out, Greene learned that Cornwallis had been reinforced to 5,000 men and decided against an attempt. In a long letter to Washington on November 24, Greene justified his position. He had only 3,000 men exclusive of militia: "I cannot promise myself Victory, nor even a Prospect of it, with Inferior Numbers. The Cause is too important to be trifled with to shew our Courage, and your Character too deeply interested to sport away upon unmilitary Principles." Greene offered to attack if Washington so wished. The commander in chief did not, and Greene crossed the Delaware again on November 29, marching to join Washington at Whitemarsh, Pennsylvania.

CHAPTER SIX

THE WIDENED WAR

ON DECEMBER 3, 1777, A DELEGATION FROM CONGRESS arrived in Washington's camp at Whitemarsh to press for offensive action against the British in Philadelphia. Washington asked his generals to respond in writing. Greene, now much more the realist, wrote Washington a very long letter, concluding as follows:

> However desirable the destruction of General Howe's army may be and however impatient the public may be for this desirable event, I cannot recommend the measure. I have taken the most serious View of the subject in every point in which I am able to examine it and cannot help thinking the probability of a disappointment is infinitely greater than of Success. We must not be governed in our measures by our Wishes. The love of glory natural to men often prompts them to exceed the bounds of human nature in their enterprizes.

Shortly thereafter Washington moved the army from Whitemarsh to a location nearer to Philadelphia. Known as Valley Forge, it was on the Schuylkill River some twenty-five miles from the city. The troops arrived there on December 19 and were soon at work building some one thousand small huts to serve as living quarters. There the army passed a terrible winter, although suffering was actually worse at Morristown, New Jersey, in the winter of 1779–80.

Conditions at Valley Forge during the winter of 1777–78 were appalling. At first, tents were the only shelter; weeks passed with no meat, and there were few vegetables and often nothing to drink save water. The basic food was something called fire cake, consisting of bread baked on a stove. Soap was also scarce, leaving the men prey to disease. Even fuel was in short supply. The 4,000 men at Valley Forge were so poorly clothed that they hardly dared venture outside their windowless huts. Early February 1778 brought bitter cold and snow. As many as 2,500 Americans died at Valley Forge, while many others deserted. The suffering of the troops was, however, not so much due to the weather as to the inefficiency of the commissariat services, and because Americans were unwilling to expend the resources to support their troops in the field, even as some citizens were selling provisions to the British in Philadelphia for gold. Meanwhile, the various state governments consistently failed to meet the quotas of supplies set by the Congress.

This coincided with serious unrest among some of the army's most influential generals, in what became known as the "Conway Cabal." It followed on the heels of Washington's defeats on the Brandywine and at Germantown, and the loss of the Delaware forts, coupled with Gates's triumph at Saratoga. Although details remain obscure, a number of disgruntled generals, centered on

Conway but including quartermaster general and former member of the Continental Congress Brigadier General Thomas Mifflin, intrigued with Gates in an effort to convince Congress to remove Washington and replace him with Gates. This resonated because many influential figures, particularly politicians outside the army, were frustrated by the string of defeats and unaware of the true situation. Key figures outside the army opposed to Washington (and Greene) included Benjamin Rush and James Lovell. The opposition did not understand that the victory at Saratoga owed little to Gates but was rather the culmination of General Schuyler's scorched-earth policies and Benedict Arnold's inspired leadership. Greene, who well understood this, wrote General Alexander McDougall that Gates was a "mere child of fortune" who had happened to be in the right place at the right time. He noted that "the foundation of all the Northern success was laid long before his arrival there; and Arnold and Lincoln were the principal instruments in completing the work."

Although no doubt his feelings were prompted in large part by his own loyalty to Washington, Greene's view is shared by most historians. Still, the plotters accused Washington of being a weak leader and indecisive. Greene knew that he too had come under heavy criticism for his performance at Germantown. This only served to draw him closer to Washington. Greene certainly had no love for Conway and protested his promotion by Congress to major general in December 1777 to no avail.

Mifflin in particular disliked Greene, believing him to be incompetent and overly cautious. Greene was well aware of this, noting, "General Mifflin and his creatures have been endeavoring too wound my reputation. It is said I govern the Genl and do every thing to damp the spirit of enterprise."

Even before the army had moved to Valley Forge, Congress revived the Board of War in order to reassert authority over the army that it had abandoned in late 1776, in part at Greene's urging. Mifflin secured appointment to the new board, and, in the worst possible circumstance for the army's commander in chief, resigned his post of quartermaster general. Mifflin also proposed expanding the board to five members and nominated Gates to be its president. Congress also named Conway as the army's inspector general and promoted him to major general. In this new post, Conway would be expected to visit all Continental Army camps and installations and would thus be in perfect position to sow unrest against the commander in chief.

The plotters seemed well on the way to toppling Washington. Although some claimed that Conway and company never went beyond criticism, Greene for one never doubted that their intent was to remove Washington, and that he would soon follow. Greene summed up to McDougall that a "faction . . . is said to be forming under the auspices of General Gates and General Mifflin, to supplant his Excellency from the command of the Army and get Genl Gates at the head of it."

Ultimately those involved in the Conway Cabal misread their own influence and came up against the absolute loyalty of most of the army to Washington. By the spring of 1779, the effort to replace Washington had run its course. The Board of War lost any position of influence and Conway and Mifflin were in effect shelved, never again to enjoy influence. Gates ultimately penned a letter of apology to Washington. Ultimately the man known to much of the uninformed public as the "hero of Saratoga" received another major command from Congress, with most unfortunate consequences for the Patriot cause.

While Valley Forge saw terrible suffering and intrigue that winter, it also brought a better-trained army, for at the beginning of December 1777 Frederick Wilhelm August Hendrik Ferdinand Steuben, self-styled Baron von Steuben, arrived in America and soon had made his way to the encampment. Steuben volunteered to serve as drillmaster to the Continental Army. Although presenting himself as a lieutenant general in the army of Prussian King Frederick II (the Great), he had in truth been only a captain. Washington immediately recognized Steuben's talents and put him to work.

Capable of swearing great oaths in many languages, Steuben was a colorful character who knew how to motivate men, and with Washington's blessing immediately set to work to train and drill the army, instilling in it a new pride and discipline. Washington subsequently appointed Steuben the army's inspector general, and in 1779 Steuben published a manual in which he greatly simplified European military drill. The Prussian army was a harsh service with brutal, even draconian discipline. To his great credit, Steuben recognized this type of discipline would not work in America, and he constantly sought to impress on the officers their responsibility to look after the well-being of their men and to explain the reasons behind their orders. After Valley Forge, Washington was able to strike at small units of the British Army and fight on equal terms with it in the field. Steuben, like Lafayette, soon became an important Greene friend and ally.

In the procurement crisis during that dreadful winter, Washington turned to Greene, asking him to become the army's quartermaster general. Greene agreed, and immediately set to work on this difficult but absolutely essential assignment. The immediate vicinity of Valley Forge had been picked clean, and Washington ordered Greene to forage more widely and take whatever was necessary. Farmers were issued certificates that supposedly would enable them to secure future compensation for the livestock and other goods seized. This was not what Washington or Greene wanted, for it alienated many Americans from the cause, but with the very survival of the army at stake, there simply was no other choice. Greene wrote Washington on February 15: "The Inhabitants cry out and beset me from all quarters, but like Pharoh I harden my heart." On February 14, Greene's men caught two civilians transporting supplies to sell to the British, and Greene ordered them each given one hundred lashes "by way of example." Such work was undoubtedly hard on all concerned. To prevent cattle, horses, and other animals starving for lack of forage, Greene ordered all animals that might be of use to the army to be confiscated. By late February, Greene's aggressive actions had greatly improved the army's supply situation.

The personal strain of Valley Forge was eased considerably for Greene when, in January 1778, Caty joined him there. Martha Washington, as well as the wives of Knox and some other officers, were also in camp. The presence of the women, who shared some of the same hardships as their husbands, seems to have had a positive effect on morale. Caty was soon again pregnant.

Congress had been considering installing General Schuyler as Mifflin's successor as quartermaster general, but a congressional committee visiting Valley Forge reached the same conclusion as had Washington: Greene was the logical and best choice. Greene neither sought not wanted the post, which would take him from field command and the recognition that he so desperately sought. Indeed, accepting it was certainly the most difficult decision of his military career. Congress had specified that he would be a staff and not a line officer, and he complained to his good friend Joseph Reed in mid-March, "I am taken out of the Line of splendor." He wrote to General McDougall, "All of you will be immortallising your selves in the golden pages of History while I am confined to a series of druggery [drudgeries] to pave the way for it." Greene wanted to win military glory, and he reportedly told Washington later, "Nobody ever heard of a quarter master in history." Not only would the assignment entail long hours of thankless work, but it would also probably mean difficulties with Congress, a body Greene held in low esteem. Clearly Greene's absolute loyalty to Washington and the latter's desire to have a trusted subordinate in that post were the factors behind Greene's decision.

In his new position Greene would be responsible for purchasing, transporting, and distributing to the army all of its supplies. He would have charge when the army was on the march and be responsible for supplies en route. He would also have to establish and oversee supply lines and depots. All of this, however, came at a time when Congress was increasingly strapped for funds and its currency was rapidly depreciating in value.

Although Greene accepted the post, he was able to secure some important concessions. Thus he retained the rank of major general and he secured a vague promise of a place on the battlefield, although he no longer had command of a division. Congress also promised him a free hand and appointment of two trusted friends as his chief subordinates. John Cox, a merchant in civilian life, would oversee the army's purchases and monitor stocks of supplies available, while Charles Pettit, a lawyer and accountant, would have control of the department's accounts.

While Greene was willing to serve for his salary as major general, Pettit and Cox wanted more because of their lucrative civilian positions. Congress offered all three men a 1 percent commission on all goods contracted for the army, to be divided however they wished. Such a procedure was common in the armies of that era, and Mifflin had enjoyed the same arrangement. Certainly, money was a consideration for Greene. He had already reached the conclusion that Americans valued it above all else, writing his brother and business partner Jacob in early February, "Money becomes more and more the Americans' object. You must get rich, or you will be of no consequence." Greene was not above self-pity, as he noted to his brother William Greene,

> I have spent but a short hour at home since the commencement of the War. . . . I have totally neglected my interest, and every measure to cultivate or increase its consequence. I have in a great degree deprivd myself of all the pleasures of domestick life. I am wearing out my constitution and the prime of life. It is true I shall have the consolation of exerting my small abilities in support of the Liberties of my Country, but that is but poor food to subsist a family upon in old Age.

Greene accepted the position on March 2, 1778. Despite his reluctance, there is no question but that he performed brilliantly in the new position. Intimately familiar with all aspects of the army and its problems, he accomplished wonders. He transformed the position of quartermaster general into one of the most important in the army, with easy access to Washington. And, as it worked out, Greene was still able on occasion to command troops in the field.

Greene's transformation of the Quartermaster Department was nothing short of amazing, especially as he accomplished it in only three months. In short order he secured sufficient numbers of tents and other necessary equipment, remedying the most glaring shortages. His deputy quartermasters were both young and competent, and he generally appointed effective individuals to staff the department. Among improvements he introduced was the practice of sending purchasing agents greater distances to secure supplies. Perhaps his most important change was in establishing well-guarded grain depots that could readily supply the army, no matter its location. These were established in widely scattered locations in New York, Pennsylvania, and New Jersey. Greene also set up arms depots, which were also dispersed. These changes and the acquisition of horses, wagons, and boats all transformed the Continental Army into a highly mobile force, able to operate wherever Washington might choose to send it. The supply system employed some three thousand people (including Greene's brother in Coventry, Jacob Greene, whom he appointed commissary agent for Rhode Island), including wagon masters and laborers, and it was absolutely essential. Greene thus insured that the army would not only survive, but would be able to fight through to final victory.

With the spring campaign season fast approaching, both sides contemplated their next moves. In early 1778, the only major British holdings were Philadelphia, New York, and Newport, Rhode Island; and, in answer to the American-French alliance, the British government decided to offer the rebellious colonies everything they had asked for, short of independence. London dispatched to Philadelphia a peace commission headed by the Earl of Carlisle. When nothing came of that effort, in early June 1778 General Howe resigned his commission and was replaced as British commander in North America by Lieutenant General Sir Henry Clinton, who immediately evacuated Philadelphia.

Washington had been aware since late May that the British were planning a general movement of some sort, and he assumed correctly that they were about to quit Philadelphia altogether. Positing a British march across New Jersey to New York, Washington wrote Philemon Dickinson, New Jersey Major General of Militia, to call up his state's militia. He also ordered Maxwell's New Jersey brigade to Mount Holly. These forces, he hoped, could harass the British, destroying bridges and building obstructions to slow their movement. Washington's assumption was correct, for on June 16 two regiments of British troops departed Philadelphia before dawn, crossing the Delaware at Cooper's Point.

The next day, June 17, Washington called a council of war. Greene, much to his delight, was included in the deliberations, despite being a staff officer. Washington informed his generals that a variety of intelligence sources led him to believe that the British were in the process of evacuating Philadelphia. He calculated British strength at 10,000 men and Continental Army strength at 12,500 men, with 11,000 of these fit for service.

Washington put to the generals a series of questions to be answered in writing. Among these were whether the Americans should attempt to attack the British in Philadelphia immediately; whether the army should remain in its present location until the British completed their evacuation or should move immediately towards the Delaware; whether some units should be detached or the entire army should be kept together in order to be able to act against the British if the right circumstances arose; and whether the army should attempt to attack the British during their march.

General Charles Lee, who had been released in a prisoner exchange on April 5 following a year and a half of British captivity, led the opposition. Lee, it turned out, proved more useful to the British while freed and with Washington than he would have been as their prisoner. Lee now argued that the British should be permitted to withdraw to New York unmolested. He reasoned that, thanks to the French alliance, American victory in the war was assured, and that it was thus unwise to risk the army in a major stand-up battle in which he believed the Continentals could not compete effectively with British regulars. Although the generals did vote to follow the British at a discreet distance, they also opposed an attack under almost any circumstances. Wayne was one of the few arguing for an immediate attack.

Greene's response was both measured and sound: "The State of European politicks and the promising condition of our own affairs forbid our taking any rash measures, or putting anything to the hazard unnecessarily. But moving toward the Delaware is neither rash nor hazardous." Greene argued for keeping the entire army together: "I would not detach from this Army, for in doing that we hazard both parts, and if it's dangerous for the whole army to go into the neighbourhood of the Enemy it must be still more for a part."

While the matter was thus under review, the last British troops departed Philadelphia on June 18, crossing the Delaware and advancing in a northeasterly direction on an easy march. New York City lay ninety miles distant. Washington broke camp at Valley Forge the next day. Thanks to Greene's previous positioning of supplies, the Americans were able to move faster than the British, who were slowed by a large supply train of some one thousand wagons. Detaching small units to harass the British, Washington sent the main portion of the army north of, and parallel to, Clinton's route. The leading American elements crossed the Delaware on June 20, but the last troops did not enter New Jersey until the evening of June 22. The next day, the British easily brushed aside a force of New Jersey militia at Crosswicks, while the main body of

Continentals entered Hopewell about twenty miles to the north. Two days later, the British reached Allentown, only fifteen miles from Washington at Hopewell.

On the morning of June 24 at Hopewell, Washington held another council of war. With time quickly running out for an attack on the British on the march, Washington asked his generals whether they would now approve an attack. Greene was in favor, but the majority, led by Lee, was still opposed. Greene then put forth a compromise: an assault by two brigades of light troops against the rear and flanks of the British column in conjunction with already positioned militia and Continental Army units. The rest of the army would remain close by in order to be able to participate if necessary. The council of war approved only 1,500 men for such an operation. Greene signed the document with the other generals, but Wayne was so disgusted by the decision that he refused. Washington was also disappointed but almost immediately received letters from both Greene and Lafayette. Greene began with an apology:

> The delicate situation I am in prevents my speaking in councils of war with that openness I should if I was to take part in the command. I must confess that the opinion I subscribed to . . . does not perfectly coincide with my Sentiments. I am not for hazzarding a general action unnecessarily but I am clearly of opinion for makeing a serious impression with the Light Troops and for haveing the Army in supporting distance.

Greene went on:

> If we suffer the enemy to pass through the Jerseys without attempting anything upon them, I think we shall ever regret it. I cannot help but thinking we magnify our difficulties beyond

> realities. . . . I think we can make a very serious impression without any great risque, and if it should amount to a general action I think the chance is greatly in our favor. However I think we can make a partial attack without suffering them to bring us to a general action.

Lafayette went further. In his letter to Washington he suggested that he, Greene, Steuben, Wayne, and two brigadier generals were in agreement that Washington should employ 2,500 men in the attack rather than 1,500. Lafayette even chided Washington for having called the council. Now for once, Washington decided to override one of his councils and to send not the 1,500 men agreed to by his generals or the 2,500 recommended by Lafayette, but rather 4,000 men. The army as a whole would also be relocated closer to the British.

Clinton, meanwhile, had concluded that it was too dangerous to continue his march toward New Brunswick into terrain that would force him to string out his army and make it more vulnerable to American attack, and also to risk encountering northern forces under Gates. Instead, on the morning of June 25 he changed the direction of his march to move through Monmouth County to high ground at Middletown. There he would be able to control an evacuation from Sandy Hook. The route would take his army through Monmouth Court House.

On June 25, Washington left his tents and heavy baggage behind at Hopewell and moved the army seven miles to Rocky Hill. This put the Americans on a converging line with the British. With a major engagement now imminent, Washington offered the command of the advance element to Lee, the senior general in the army next to Washington himself. Lee declined, whereupon Washington gave it to Lafayette. But when Lee learned that the command actually approached half the strength of the army, he requested the command be shifted to him, and Washington agreed. This meant that Lee now commanded an operation he had strongly opposed. The shift in command was one of the major mistakes of Washington's military career.

Lee commanded some 5,000 men near Englishtown, while on the night of June 25 Washington moved the rest of the army from Kingston to Cranbury. Washington issued explicit orders to Lee to attack the rear of the English column the next day. He also instructed Lee to call a council of war and there issue precise orders to his subordinates regarding the plan of attack. While Lee did indeed call the meeting, he merely told his commanders that he had no set plan and that they should await his battlefield orders.

The Battle of Monmouth Court House (or simply Monmouth) in New Jersey was really two separate engagements fought on the same day. The battle began about 8 a.m., several miles north of Monmouth Court House, when Lee's 5,000 men with twelve guns attacked the rear portion of the British column, spread out over some twelve miles. The fighting occurred in intense heat (perhaps more than one hundred degrees Fahrenheit) and clouds of dust. The high temperature claimed a number of dead on both sides from heat exhaustion and sunstroke. Unknown to Washington, Clinton had strengthened his rear guard with some of his best troops and had given command there to Cornwallis.

The battle opened when Wayne's men skirmished with the British. With no other option, Clinton turned and engaged the Americans. Lee, meanwhile, showed great caution and soon lost control of the situation, ordering units about in such fashion as to completely confuse his subordinates. After several hours of this, Lee's units began to withdraw piecemeal. An angry Washington, seeing troops streaming past, could not understand what had transpired, and tradition has him swearing great oaths. He then rode forward and demanded an explanation from Lee, who could not explain his actions other than to say that he thought it was not a good idea to fight a major engagement with the British at the time. A furious Washington told Lee that he expected his orders to be obeyed.

Washington then took control of the battle himself, in effect directing the Continental defense against the British counterattack, the second phase of the battle. Greene played a key role in this. At the beginning of the battle, Greene had remained with Washington, but in temporary command of Lee's division on the American right, ready to move into action should the attack become a general engagement. Indeed, before the Americans had retreated, Washington had ordered Greene forward to support the attack, but as soon as Greene learned that Lee was retreating, he withdrew to be able to contain the British advance. Twice, Greene's men drove back furious British counterattacks, holding until the disorganized and retreating American left could be reorganized.

This second phase of the battle saw perhaps 7,000 British troops attack the 12,000 Continentals. Washington positioned the main American line behind a hedgerow. Fighting was intense and in places man-to-man, with the Americans performing well against the attacking British, even with the bayonet. While the American center and left held, Washington sent Greene, on the right, south around to the British left flank. The British then withdrew. Washington wanted to pursue, but his men were too spent from the battle and the heat. Clinton retired to Middletown and then Sandy Hook, where the British were lifted off by ship to New York City.

The Battle of Monmouth Court House ended as a Continental victory, but it was not the outcome that Washington had hoped for or expected. Continental Army losses were 152 killed and 300 wounded for a total of 452; British losses were 290 killed, 390 wounded, and 576 captured, for a total of 1,156 casualties. Lee's actions during the battle were such as to cause many in the army to think that he might have been actively working for the British. Indeed, there is some suggestion that he had turned traitor while a British prisoner. Following the battle, however, Lee demanded a court of inquiry. Found guilty of misconduct, he resigned his commission.

Monmouth Court House was the largest single day's battle of the war. It was also the last general engagement in the North. Although there would be small engagements thereafter, the northern theater settled into stalemate and remained thus until the end of the war.

Following the battle, Washington moved the army toward the Hudson to be able to keep close watch on Clinton. Greene had charge of the march. The army arrived in New Brunswick on July 4, 1778, and Greene rode on ahead to select a more permanent location. He found it in White Plains, where the army camped on July 21.

Greene was unhappy in his assignment. We shall never know just how sincere he was in occasional letters to his brother Jacob and cousin Griffin, where he threatened to quit the army so that he might return to Caty and the children he did not know and enter into the pursuit of wealth; but clearly he was not pleased when Washington sent him a terse note complaining of "neglect" in the affairs of the quartermaster's office and telling him that he needed to confer with him personally before writing to French Vice Admiral Jean Baptiste Charles Henri Hector Theodat, Comte d'Estaing about a siege of New York. This prompted a letter from Greene at White Plains. Blunt and laced with self-pity, it was unlike any letter Greene had ever sent to Washington. He began as follows: "Your Excellency has made me very unhappy. I can submit very patient to deserved censure, but it wounds my feelings exceedingly to meet with a rebuke for doing what I conceived to be a proper part of my duty, and in the order of things." He said he had carried out his duty of finding the best possible site for the army to camp, to the detriment of his own health, and he went on to remind Washington of his effective service to him and to the nation. Then he came to the heart of the matter, raising an issue that obviously still rankled nearly a year later: "I have never been troublesome to your Excellency to publish any thing to my advantage altho I think myself as justly entitled as some others who have been more fortunate. Particularly in the action of Brandywine." Since it was apparent that Washington was displeased with his work, Greene offered to resign: "As I came to the quarter masters department with reluctance so I shall leave it with pleasure. Your influence brought me in and the want of your approbation will induce me to go out."

Reading this almost pitiful letter from Greene must have been difficult for Washington, who was often distant and not given to displays of emotion. Clearly he had not planned to offend Greene, whose services were so important to the cause and whose advice and support he so greatly valued. Washington immediately replied: "I shall assure you, that you retain the same hold of my affections I have professed to allow you. . . . I have ever been happy in your friendship, and have no scruples in declaring that I think myself indebted to your Abilities, honour and candour, to your attachment to me, and your faithful Services to the Public." Washington gently reminded Greene that friendship must not "debar" frank discussions of the needs of the army and, when he could find nobody in Greene's department available, he thought it only correct to bring this to Greene's attention. Washington concluded, "But let me beseech you my dear Sir not to harbor any distrusts of my friendship, or conceive that I meant to wound the feelings of a Person whom I greatly esteem and regard."

On August 2, Washington followed up this letter with one to Congress fulsome in praise of Greene for the transformation he had effected in the quartermaster general's office. These two letters had the desired result. Greene returned to his work with enthusiasm.

Washington had hoped that with French assistance he might move against New York. He received word that a French squadron of twelve ships of the line under d'Estaing transporting 4,000 troops, had arrived off the New England coast. The British then had only nine ships of the line at New York, but on July 9 d'Estaing tried and failed in an effort to get his large ships across the bar. D'Estaing and Washington then agreed that the Americans and French would mount an attack against Newport, Rhode Island, in their first joint operation of the war. Washington ordered Greene to set to work moving reinforcements and supplies there. Unhappy with the speed of communications back and forth, Washington turned to Greene, who solved the problem with a system of dispatch riders.

At Providence, Rhode Island, Greene's friend John Sullivan had command of some 1,000 Continentals, and Washington ordered him to call out all the state militia. Washington also sent a division under Lafayette, and, as a result of Greene's lobbying, agreed on

July 24 to let him command a division there. Charles Pettit would assume Greene's quartermaster duties in his absence.

Three years after the start of the war, Greene was returning home, hopefully as a liberator. He arrived in Coventry on July 30, the first time his family had been together. Young George was now four and Martha three. Caty was also within a month of giving birth to their third child, Cornelia. Following a week at home with his family, Greene made his way to the American camp at Tiverton east of Newport, across the Sakonnet River.

Sullivan now had at his disposal about 10,000 men, a large number of whom were unreliable militia, including many New Englanders under the command of the former president of the Continental Congress, John Hancock. Among the army units present was an all-black regiment commanded by Nathanael Greene's cousin, Christopher Greene. Although southerners were appalled by this, the Rhode Islanders had insisted on it and had offered to purchase the freedom of any qualified blacks who were willing to join. The unit numbered about 150 men, the first all-black regiment in the American army, and its men fought in the front lines rather than being assigned menial tasks.

Sullivan's plan called for the Americans to cross the Sakonnet from Tiverton to Aquidneck Island (officially known as Rhode Island, but not to be confused with the state of Rhode Island) north of Newport. The Americans would move south down the east side of the island, with Greene commanding the right, Lafayette the left, and Sullivan the center. At the same time 4,000 French were to come ashore on Conanicut Island in Narragansett Bay to the west of Newport and be ferried across to Aquidneck to move south in concert with the Americans against the British garrison of some 3,000 men commanded by Major General Sir Robert Pigot. The

Americans hoped that, with French ships controlling the bay, the British would be trapped and forced to surrender.

The landings were scheduled to occur on August 10, but when he learned that the British had evacuated the Rhode Island fort opposite Tiverton, Sullivan moved the day before without informing the French. Although he was a staunch Patriot who was highly regarded by Washington, Sullivan did not always show the best judgment, and the tone of his messages to d'Estaing had already served to dampen the Frenchman's enthusiasm for the enterprise. However, that very afternoon, August 9, British Admiral Howe's squadron of thirteen warships sailed to Narraganset Bay to challenge d'Estaing's twelve warships. Because the French ships were both larger and threw a heavier weight of broadside, d'Estaing was confident of success. He promptly took his men back aboard and sailed out to meet Howe. Sullivan, hoping for d'Estaing's speedy return, marched south toward Newport.

Unfortunately for Sullivan, a violent, two-day summer storm mauled both squadrons, and d'Estaing returned only to send word to Sullivan that he was sailing to Boston to refit. This left the American land force on Aquidneck Island bereft of naval support. Greene and Lafayette met personally with d'Estaing aboard his flagship, the ship of the line *Languedoc*. Greene pleaded with d'Estaing to delay, if only for forty-eight hours, assuring d'Estaing that the French ships could then be repaired at Providence; but the French admiral was adamant, fearful that his damaged ships might be trapped in the bay by a British return. Greene's discomfort in the meeting was heightened by a bout of seasickness.

D'Estaing departed for Boston on the night of August 21. Both Greene and Sullivan were critical of the Frenchman's decision, but Greene understood the absolute importance of the French alliance, whereas Sullivan's intemperate angry statements accusing the French of treachery and cowardice served only to threaten future allied cooperation. Yet Greene, not wishing to offend his colleague, unwisely signed an extraordinarily impolitic letter to d'Estaing on August 22, which became public. To his credit, Lafayette had refused to sign and in fact sent his own letter to d'Estaing condemning it.

When the American militia saw the French ships depart, taking with them essential artillery support, thousands lost heart and themselves left. Within days, Sullivan found himself with only 5,000 men. Although he told his men that they could defeat the British without the French, Greene knew otherwise.

Sullivan withdrew somewhat to the north of Aquidneck Island and deployed his men in a two-mile-long line, with Greene commanding the right wing. There Pigot launched an attack in the early morning of August 29, in what became known as the Battle of Rhode Island. Four small British warships came up and began shelling Greene's right, but Greene shifted some of his artillery and drove them off. Greene's men also defeated a British attack and then launched a counterattack in which the Rhode Island black soldiers particularly distinguished themselves against Hessian troops, fighting with the bayonet and bare hands. The Americas held against repeated British assaults. By late afternoon, the battle ended in a draw. The Americans had suffered 211 casualties, the British 260. The Americans had fought well, but on the night of August 30, Sullivan withdrew from the island to Tiverton. It was a wise decision, for only a day later, 4,000 British reinforcements arrived under Clinton.

Sullivan continued to speak against the French over the affair, leading Washington to call on Greene to restore harmony and an effective working arrangement with the French. Washington also called on Greene to do all that he could to keep Sullivan's remarks from becoming public, and Greene was able to prevent letters by Sullivan that were critical of d'Estaing from being read in the Rhode Island legislature, then meeting in East Greenwich. He also wrote personally to d'Estaing, who graciously replied that he had not been personally insulted by Sullivan's remarks and thanked Greene for his letter, which "was of a nature to console me."

Greene returned to Coventry to visit his family again but departed before Caty gave birth, traveling to Boston to place army orders there for shoes and clothing. This work completed, Greene was returning to Coventry on September 24, when he received word that Caty had given birth the day before to their third child, a girl named Cornelia Lott Greene. Neither mother nor daughter were doing well, and Greene rode through the night to join them. In the days that followed, both showed marked improvement, and Greene soon left to return to army headquarters.

Greene's correspondence reveals the depth of his ongoing frustration over the quartermaster assignment. He knew the work was vital, but he was sensitive to the criticism that came with it. He yearned to assume a field command, preferably one in the South, where the war had now shifted.

Meanwhile, it was time for the army to go into winter encampment, and, following several weeks of searching, Greene decided on Middlebrook in central New Jersey as the site for the army's main camp. Caty arrived there in December. At Middlebrook the army passed a quiet winter. Greene continued to experience frustrations over army supply, abetted by the rapid depreciation of the currency and the corresponding yet understandable reluctance of merchants to contract with the army for the supplies and equipment necessary to keep it in the field.

In late December, Washington and Greene traveled to Philadelphia to meet with members of Congress over the situation. What was to have been a short visit turned into a stay of six weeks. The two generals conferred with the representatives on everything from strategy to supply problems. Caty was with Greene and evidently greatly enjoyed the many dinners and balls. Although Greene seems to have attended them all, he also found frustrating and even offensive the lavish scale and expense of the entertainments, especially with memories of Valley Forge so fresh. He wrote his friend General James Varnum in February 1779, "I dine'd at one table where they was an hundred and Sixty dishes; and at several others not far behind. The Growing avarice, and a declining currency, are poor materials to build our Independence upon."

Greene, of course, had to attend to the work of his department even while in Philadelphia, and there was always considerable correspondence. He and Washington also conferred on military strategy, with Washington increasingly favoring a descent on New York. They also considered a military operation against Indian tribes allied with the British in upstate New York. Greene urged the destruction of their crops rather than any effort to bring the natives to battle. He would later provide logistical support for a massive operation in the summer of 1779 commanded by Sullivan, during which soldiers destroyed some forty Iroquois villages, including a large Cayuga settlement near present-day Ithaca, New York, and burned thousands of bushels of grain.

Washington and Greene accomplished little during their stay in Philadelphia, and Congress rejected Greene's request that the

1 percent commission on army purchases be eliminated in favor of a straight salary for Pettit and Cox. His proposed payment of £3000 to each was apparently too high. Congress also continued to ignore Greene's appeals for greater funding. Frustration built. To James Deane, head of the Board of Treasury, Greene wrote that "while I am drudging in an Office from which I shall receive no honor, and very few thanks I am looseing an opportunity of doing justice to my military character. And what adds to my mortification is, that my present humiliating employment is improv'd to pave the way for others glory."

Greene was so frustrated during a second trip to Philadelphia in April 1779 that he wrote Washington and again threatened to resign unless Congress gave him the authority to transform the system. Washington penned a sympathetic response and wrote: "Your own judgement must direct. If it points to a resignation of your present office, and your inclination leads you to the southward, my wishes shall accompany it; and if the appointment of a successor to General Lincoln is left to me, I shall not hesitate in preferring you to this command, but I have little expectation of being consulted on the occasion." Benjamin Lincoln, who commanded at Charleston, was said to be suffering from the effects of a leg wound incurred in the Battle of Saratoga. As Washington feared, however, when the time came to replace Lincoln, Congress made the decision without consulting him.

Soon after Greene's return from Philadelphia, the British sent a detachment north from New York City to capture the American posts at Stony Point and Verplanck's Point. Afraid that the British were about to embark on a major drive up the Hudson, in late May Washington announced his intention to relocate the army's main camp northward. Greene then rode north to find a desirable location. When he did so, Caty, who was again pregnant, departed with their son George to return to Rhode Island.

By mid-June 1779, the army had relocated to New Windsor, New York, and was thus better placed to defend the Hudson if need be, but there was in fact little activity in the North for the remainder of the war. There were notable exceptions. One occurred on July 15, 1779, when General Wayne led 1,350 men in a night attack against a 700-man British garrison at Stony Point, twenty-five miles from New York City. This well-planned assault was carried out with unloaded muskets and bayonets. The surprised defenders promptly surrendered. Although Wayne had to abandon the post several days later, the attack secured much-needed arms and supplies. Then on August 19, Major Henry Lee led a successful attack on another New Jersey British outpost, Paulus Hook, now known as Jersey City. In a pre-dawn assault, the Continentals stormed and took the British works, killing 50 of the enemy and taking 158 prisoners, including 9 officers, for only 2 men killed and 3 wounded. The Americans immediately withdrew, leaving the British in possession of the fort and its cannon. Both raids had little military impact, but they were a considerable boost to Continental morale.

The Battle of Paulus Hook ended active military hostilities between Washington and Clinton in 1779. Washington fortified West Point, while Clinton, anticipating a shift in operations to the American South, abandoned Rhode Island. Meanwhile, good news came to the Continental cause in the form of Spain entering the war against England, although the motivation was chiefly the recovery of Gibraltar.

The lull in the fighting allowed Greene an opportunity to refocus some attention on his personal affairs. Indeed, a good bit of

Greene's surviving correspondence of 1779 and 1780 is devoted to personal financial matters. Greene biographer Theodore Thayer calculated that Greene received some $170,000 in commissions during the time he was quartermaster of the army. With the Continental dollar in free-fall, however, Greene sought investment opportunities before these sums became totally worthless. Toward that end, in April 1779 Greene formed a business association with Colonel Jeremiah Wadsworth, commissary general of the army from April 1778 to December 1779, and with businessman Barnabas Deane.

Anxious to avoid any hint of impropriety, both Greene and Wadsworth kept their dealings with Deane secret, and both communicated with him in code. Greene and Wadsworth each invested £10,000 in the firm, known as Barnabas Deane & Company. As with Jacob Greene & Company, Barnabas Deane & Company invested in privateers, but unlike the other firm, it did not have any dealings with the Quartermaster Department.

Greene also purchased land in Rhode Island, in New Jersey, and in the Hudson Valley area. He and his assistant Charles Pettit also independently invested in privateers and were part owners of Balsto Iron Works in New Jersey. Many of these investments turned out badly, and two years after its formation, Barnabas Deane & Co. was worth only £5,000.

Greene was now coming under increasing criticism in Congress for his handling of the quartermaster's office. This was not because his own family firm, Jacob Greene & Company, was in business with the department, or because Greene had personal business transactions with some of the contractors, but simply because the amounts involved were vast and accounting procedures scanty. The department was spending on the order of $500,000 a month, albeit in highly depreciated Continental currency. A vast sum for the day, this money went to some three thousand employees, and while most were honest, a number were corrupt or incompetent or both. There is absolutely no evidence that Greene ever profited from the transactions of his department beyond that which was allowed, but there is no question that a number of his agents did, and, indeed, criminal charges came to be leveled against some.

While members of Congress made a point of praising Greene for his work and integrity, they also asked to see his accounts and sidestepped the general's authority by authorizing individual states to dismiss those agents suspected of corruption or incompetence. The prideful Greene took this as an attack on his honor.

All this served to remind Greene, if he needed such, of his desire to return to field command. Following a called council of war between Washington and his senior commanders at West Point on July 2, 1779, Greene wrote letters to a dozen of his brother generals, asking them if he did not have the right to hold a field command while at the same time serving as quartermaster general. Greene was disappointed in the responses. While half of the generals agreed with him, they were either his friends or were of greater seniority than he and thus would not be threatened if he were to be given a command. The others disagreed. Nonetheless, Greene took his case to Washington, who, however, sided with the dissenters. While praising Greene's contributions, Washington ruled that Greene did not have the right to hold a field command while also serving as quartermaster general.

Greene was also concerned over, and depressed about, his family situation. In August 1779, the children were in poor health, and so was Caty, again pregnant. She wrote to Greene to complain of bleeding at the mouth and of stomach pains. Greene wrote a long letter in reply, telling her how he longed to be with his family in

Rhode Island, and that if he were there, "How tenderly would I nurse you. How attentively would I watch my sweet Angel."

Frustration over his position as quartermaster general continued to build, and on December 12, 1779, Greene submitted his resignation. Congress chose to ignore it. Then in mid-month, the 10,000–11,000 members of Washington's army began clearing land and building huts in an encampment near Morristown, New Jersey. The location was selected in large part for its close proximity both to New York City and to the Hudson River Valley. Spread over six hundred acres, the camp included some one thousand small huts, 12 men to each. That winter at Morristown would be the army's most difficult, surpassing even Valley Forge.

The weather was the coldest of the war; the waters around New York City froze, and so did part of Chesapeake Bay. Compounding matters, the Continental dollar had lost most of its value, and farmers refused to sell their produce for worthless paper. Although both Washington and Greene despised doing so, the army did have the power simply to requisition what it needed and did so. Greene, at least, had comfortable quarters in a local home. He needed this, for Caty had left the children with relatives, and, despite being close to giving birth, decided in what was now established procedure to join Greene in camp.

Heavy snows found much of the army still in tents. With roads impassable, the army was soon starving. There were days when the soldiers had no food at all. Continental Army Private Joseph Plumb Martin, whose diary forms one of the most remarkable accounts of the war, wrote of Morristown: "We are absolutely, literally starved. I do solemnly declare that I did not put a single morsel of victuals into my mouth for four days and as many nights, except a little black birch bark which I gnawed off a stick of wood, if that can be called victuals. I saw several of the men roast their old shoes and eat them. . . ."

Both Washington and Greene believed that the situation at Morristown was such that the very survival of the army and even the revolution itself were in jeopardy. Greene wrote Colonel Benoni Hathaway, a prominent militia commander and resident of Morristown, on January 6, 1780: "The Army is upon the eve of disbanding for want of Provisions, the poor soldiers having been several days without. . . . Provision is scarce at best; but the late terrible storm and the depth of the Snow and the drifts in the Roads, prevent the little stock coming forward which is in readiness at the distant Magazines." Greene called on the militia to assist by getting out teams to open the road to Hackettstown some twenty-five miles distant where there were provisions. "The Roads must be kept open by the Inhabitants or the Army cannot be subsisted. And unless the good people immediately lend their assistance to foreward supplies the Army must disband."

Some relief came in mid-January when the storms abated, and Washington allowed himself at least to think about offensive operations. He again turned to Greene to help him plan an attack while the rivers were still frozen solid. Greene proposed moving 2,500 men across the ice from Morristown against the British on Staten Island. Toward that end, he secured some five-hundred sleighs and sleds from the surrounding countryside on the pretense of using them to secure provisions.

Major General William Alexander, Lord Stirling, led the attack on the night of January 14–15. Unfortunately for the Americans, the British learned of the raid in time and were able to hold them off. After twenty-four hours on Staten Island, Stirling retired with only a handful of prisoners and some captured stores.

Unfortunately for the cause, a number of New Jersey civilians joined the expedition in the guise of militiamen and then looted and plundered on Staten Island. Although Washington ordered all stolen property that could be recovered turned over to British authorities, much harm had been done. Days later, the British retaliated by attacking Newark and burning the academy there, as well as the courthouse and the meetinghouse at Elizabethtown.

Hyperinflation, meanwhile, rendered the Continental currency all but worthless. Farmers and merchants were reluctant to contract to sell goods to the government at one price when they would be paid later in inflated currency worth far less; and Quartermaster Department personnel, who were paid wages on a percentage of the transactions, and who appeared to be making vast sums, were in fact making next to nothing.

Seemingly unable to halt the inflation, Congress came up with a new means of obtaining army supplies: a system of quotas of various goods for each state to supply. As an incentive, if a state met its quota, two-thirds of the money owed by the state to Congress and the war effort would be forgiven. This did not work as intended. States were tardy in making such shipments, did not meet the quantities specified, or, in the worst cases, did not make any shipments at all. Worse for Greene, if a state's quota called for a specific item to be provided, then the army was forbidden from purchasing these items in that state.

Congress concluded that the new system would allow it to reduce the Quartermaster Department in size, while at the same time increasing the accountability of its officers. Greene strongly disagreed. In letters to Congress, he took the position that the plan had originated with a group of congressional delegates who were plotting his downfall. In mid-January 1781, Greene sent a letter to the president of Congress, Samuel Huntington, pointing out that he had submitted his resignation as army quartermaster general a month earlier but had heard nothing. Again, Congress did not respond directly. It did establish a committee to reorganize the Quartermaster Department, but Greene's enemy Thomas Mifflin was among its members.

Meanwhile, on January 31 Caty gave birth to a son, Nathanael Ray Greene. As delighted as Greene was by this happy event, he also was facing monumental problems related to supply, and now decided to go to Philadelphia in person. Less than a week in the capital convinced him that Congress would not advance the money necessary to fight another campaign. He wrote a curt message to Huntington, telling him of his disappointment and that he was tired of meetings and the failure of Congress to pass a resolution expressing its confidence in the quartermaster's integrity. He said he would leave Philadelphia immediately.

Such behavior did not win Greene friends in Congress. Indeed, in a private session, when his friends introduced a resolution supporting him, it failed to win approval. Greene departed Philadelphia on April 10, 1780. He summed up his feelings in a letter of April 25 to Joseph Reed, president of the Pennsylvania council: "I feel my self so soured, and hurt, at the ungenerous, as well as illiberal treatment of Congress, and the different Boards, that it will be impossible for me to do business with them, with proper temper; and besides I have lost all confidence in the justice and rectitude of their intentions."

Greene returned to Morristown to find the situation dire. The army's misery continued well past the last of the snow in early April. The currency was all but worthless, food and basic equipment were in short supply, and the men had not been paid for months (not that their pay would have purchased anything of value). The situation was near mutiny, and in late May two regiments of the Connecticut Line threatened just that. Then came news of disaster in the South where, with the surrender of Charleston, the Continental Army experienced its most catastrophic defeat of the entire war.

With General Clinton preparing to return to New York from the South, leaving the able Cornwallis to continue the campaign there, General Knyphausen, who commanded in New York in Clinton's absence, planned his own operation in New Jersey. Believing that the people of that state were weary of the long war and that militia would switch sides and the weakened Continental Army forces might easily be defeated, on June 6 Knyphausen crossed with 5,000 men from Staten Island to Elizabethtown, then moved inland toward the community of Connecticut Farms. His goal was to capture strategic Hobart Gap, enabling him to march on the American headquarters in Morristown. Much to Knyphausen's surprise, however, the British and Hessian force encountered stout militia resistance. The attackers then burned several farms and civilian homes, but these actions only served to bring out more resistance.

Washington believed that Knyphausen's assault was not a major British effort, which he still thought would take the form of an attack up the Hudson on Clinton's return. Nonetheless, he could not allow Knyphausen to continue unchecked, and so he called on Greene to lead an attack on the night of June 8. No doubt Greene was delighted that Washington would see fit to turn to his quartermaster general for this task. Rain, however, led to the assault being called off. It did not matter, for Knyphausen, frustrated by the local response, began withdrawing to Elizabethtown that same night. Greene proceeded to the Watchung Mountains overlooking Springfield where he could monitor Knyphausen's movements. When Greene left Morristown, Caty and the new baby also departed, returning to Rhode Island by carriage.

On June 17, Clinton returned to New York with much of his expeditionary force. Knyphausen was still at Elizabethtown. Not pleased that his second-in-command had undertaken this foray without his approval, Clinton nonetheless decided to make the most of the situation, sending reinforcements to Knyphausen and ordering him to march toward Springfield, while he himself made plans to move up the Hudson. If Knyphausen could tie down Washington in a major engagement in New Jersey, Clinton would be able to move swiftly up the Hudson, take its principal fortress of West Point, and secure control of that key waterway.

Washington faced the real danger that if he shifted too many forces north to the Hudson, Clinton might then countermarch and get in behind the Americans, trapping and destroying the army and probably ending the war. Thus, when Clinton embarked a number of his men in transports and appeared to be about to move up the Hudson, Washington moved cautiously. On June 22, he put the bulk of the army in motion toward Pompton, New Jersey, just close enough to West Point to be able to react to any threat there, but not so close as to expose the American rear.

Washington left Greene in command of a small force of about 1,000 Continentals and 2,000 militia under Brigadier General Philemon Dickinson at Springfield to confront Knyphausen at Elizabethtown. Knyphausen had perhaps 5,000 infantry, some cavalry, and several guns. When Knyphausen began his movement toward Greene on June 23, Greene immediately dispatched a messenger to Washington some fifteen miles distant with the news and then deployed his forces.

As the British advanced, they were harassed by militia under General Maxwell. In the meantime, Greene detached small numbers of regulars under Major Henry Lee and Colonel Elias Dayton to harry the attackers, while Greene deployed his regulars to cover the Rahway River bridge before Springfield. Knyphausen's men advanced in two columns. The first, under Knyphausen himself, proceeded along Galloping Hill Road directly toward Springfield with the aim of fixing Greene in place, while the second under Brigadier General Edward Mathew moved to the right along Vauxhall Road with the plan of crossing the Rahway there, turning the American left, and getting in behind Greene.

The battle opened at about 11 a.m. with a British attack on Colonel Israel Angell's Rhode Island regiment defending the bridge. Lee's cavalry inflicted a number of casualties on Mathew's column but were soon forced to fall back and take up another position on the Vauxhall Road. Knyphausen meanwhile launched a series of attacks on Springfield itself over about a forty-minute period. The Americans did well but, faced with superior numbers and artillery, Greene ordered his main body to fall back, while at the same time dispatching reinforcements to support the troops on the Vauxhall Road, who then halted the British there.

Greene's main body then withdrew in good order to the high ground of Short Hills. Recognizing the strength of the new American position, Knyphausen first hesitated and then decided to withdraw. As the British retreated, they set fire to the nearly fifty houses in Springfield, burning down all but four of them. A small number of Continentals and the militia harassed the British during their withdrawal, inflicting a number of casualties and possibly ensuring the full return of the British to Staten Island.

Washington, learning of Greene's withdrawal, had ordered the army to countermarch to his aid. Clinton, however, made no move to assist Knyphausen, but rather placed in motion another plan that he expected would bring him control of West Point and the entire Hudson. The Battle of Springfield had claimed 13 Americans killed, 61 wounded, and 9 missing. British casualties are unknown but were probably on the order of 25 dead and 75 wounded.

Greene could be pleased that his men had halted a force of regulars twice his own number. Although the Battle of Springfield was hardly a major engagement, it was nonetheless an important American victory and wrote finis to British ambitions in New Jersey. Because the war now moved south, the Battle of Springfield is sometimes known as the "forgotten victory."

Following the battle, Greene rejoined Washington. Buoyed by his generalship in this well-fought battle, he was now determined to give up the post of quartermaster general and secure a major field command. In late July, Congress enacted a new plan that reduced both the salaries and the numbers of personnel in the Quartermaster Department. Greene's response was immediate. On July 26, he resubmitted his letter of resignation, and this time it was sharply worded. Greene charged that Congress had made it impossible for him to continue by firing his best assistants:

> It is unnecessary for me to go into the general objection I have to the plan. It is sufficient to say that my feelings are injured, and the officers necessary to conduct the business, are not allowed; nor is proper provision made for some of those that are. . . . My Rank is high in the line of the Army; and sacrifices on this account I have made, together with the fatigue and anxiety I have undergone, far outbalance all the emoluments I have derived from the appointment. . . .

Many in Congress were angered by Greene's letter, even to the point of suggesting that he should be removed from the army altogether. Washington was certainly not pleased that one of his senior commanders was feuding with Congress. Indeed, Congress hastened to demonstrate its control over army affairs when it named General Gates to assume Lincoln's command in the South with no input from Washington.

Washington now appealed to Congress to reconsider plans to "suspend" Greene from his command. A few days later, Congress named Colonel Timothy Pickering to succeed Greene as quartermaster general. Greene agreed to continue to serve in that post without commissions until Pickering had a chance to learn the system.

On August 3, Washington placed Major General Benedict Arnold in command of the key American fortress of West Point. Only two weeks later, on August 16, Gates and much of his army were destroyed in the Battle of Camden in South Carolina. Morale plummeted. This grim news was partially offset by the July 1780 arrival at Newport of a new French squadron carrying 5,000 troops under General Count Jean Baptiste D. de Vimeur de Rochambeau. The French also brought the welcome news that an even larger fleet was on its way.

On September 17, Washington traveled north to meet with Rochambeau and French Admiral Charles d'Arsac, chevalier de Ternay. Proof of his confidence in Greene, Washington left him in charge of the army with full authority to act in the commander in chief's absence. Washington wrote, "I have so intire confidence in your prudence and abilities, that I leave the conduct of it to your direction." He did, however, instruct Greene to avoid battle unless it could be on "advantageous terms."

The day after Washington's departure, Greene learned that British ships had been spotted off Sandy Hook, moving toward New York. He immediately sent word to Washington, who ordered that he move the army to Tappan, New Jersey, where he would be better situated to meet any possible thrust by Clinton up the Hudson against West Point. Greene insisted that the movement of September 20 be carried out in complete secrecy, and to insure this he ordered riflemen posted with orders to shoot to kill any deserters.

Washington's meeting at Hartford, while useful for allied cooperation and building trust, did not bring concrete results. The British, having recently received naval reinforcements, soon blockaded Ternay's ships at Newport, and Rochambeau informed Washington that he believed it was necessary he remain in the vicinity of the French ships. The northern theater of war remained in stalemate.

CHAPTER SEVEN

THE WAR IN THE SOUTH

THE CENTER OF THE FIGHTING HAD SHIFTED TO THE SOUTH in December 1778, the result of intervention by Secretary of State for the American Department Lord Germain in London. He had decided, without abandoning New York, to move the focus of the British military effort southward. This appealed for several reasons. That region had a larger Loyalist following, and it was in close proximity to British bases in the West Indies. The British already held Florida, taken from Spain after the French and Indian War. Their plan was to secure Georgia, then the Carolinas, and finally Virginia. Germain believed that the isolation of the northern states would lead to their collapse through sheer exhaustion.

Opposition to the war was in fact growing in Britain, and increasingly the British government found itself justifying the costly war on the grounds that Britain had made a commitment to defend loyal Americans against rebel vengeance and could thus not abandon them. An eighteenth-century domino theory also held sway. When Prime Minister Lord North asked George III whether the war was worth the cost, the king rebuked him with the statement that were America to wrest its independence from Britain, it would inevitably lead to the loss, bit by bit, of the entire British empire, including Ireland.

The British campaign in the South opened with success. On December 29, 1778, the British captured Savannah, and by the end of February 1779, they controlled all Georgia. In June 1779, British Major General Augustine Prevost led an attack on Charleston, South Carolina, but met failure. The Americans were intent on expelling the British from Savannah, but, recognizing their inability to do this by themselves, called on the French, and Admiral d'Estaing, then in the West Indies, agreed to assist. In mid-September, d'Estaing landed 3,500 men eight miles south of Savannah, and General Benjamin Lincoln joined him with 1,500 Continentals and militia. Prevost, however, rejected an allied call for surrender, and the Americans opened siege operations and began to shell the city on October 4.

Weeks of delay had allowed the British, assisted by slave labor, to strengthen the Savannah defenses, and when at last the attack occurred on October 9, it failed with heavy French and American casualties: 244 dead and 584 wounded as opposed to British losses of only 40 killed and 63 wounded. D'Estaing was unwilling to try again and returned with his fleet to France. Washington, who had been counting on d'Estaing in any operation against New York City, now was forced to scuttle his own plans.

In early 1780, Clinton took advantage of d'Estaing's departure to put together the largest British expeditionary force since Howe's operation against Philadelphia in 1777. On February 11, 1780, some

14,000 British troops began coming ashore on Johns Island, thirty miles south of Charleston. A month later, on March 19, Clinton laid siege to that city.

Lincoln and the entire American army in the South took up position in Charleston; Lincoln, having agreed to an appeal from the city and state leaders, allowed his forces to be bottled up there. But as soon as the first British shells began to fall on Charleston, the same leaders demanded he surrender. The city capitulated on May 12, 1780. The loss was staggering. At Charleston, the British captured 5,466 officers and men (including 7 generals), 400 cannon, and 6 small warships. It was the biggest single defeat for American arms of the entire war and the greatest defeat for an American army before the fall of Bataan in 1942.

Clinton believed that the rest of South Carolina must now inevitably submit, and he returned to New York in early June, leaving behind in the South General Cornwallis and 8,500 men. At the same time, Congress appointed Gates to command what remained of the Southern Army. Gates joined Major General Johann de Kalb at Coxe's Mill, North Carolina, on July 25. The army was short of food and in no condition for offensive operations, but instead of taking time to reorganize his forces and restore morale, Gates immediately set out with just 4,000 men—only about 1,500 of them regulars—on a reckless 120-mile march to seize the British post at Camden, South Carolina, held by Lieutenant Colonel Francis, Lord Rawdon, who at once called on Cornwallis for assistance.

Cornwallis hurried up from Charleston with some 3,000 men, 800 of whom succumbed to the intense summer heat. He arrived at Camden on August 13, and on August 16 he attacked with his 2,200 men. Gates had 3,000. In the ensuing battle, the American militia broke and ran. Although the regulars of the Delaware and Maryland line stood and fought bravely under the able de Kalb, who was ultimately killed, Gates was routed. The British captured all his artillery, baggage, and supplies, and a great number of his muskets and ammunition. Gates himself rode 60 miles in one day, and 180 in three all the way to Hillsboro to avoid capture.

Greene would write of Gates and Camden, "No man but he in America, has the faculty of taking and loseing whole Armies. His retreat is equal to that of Zenophon but only a little more rapid." Yet in January 1781, having experienced army command himself, Greene could reflect to Alexander Hamilton when writing about Gates: "What little incidents either give or destroy reputation. How many long hours a man may labour with an honest zeal in his Countrys service and be disgraced for the most triffling error in conduct or opinion. . . . Therefore it is necessary for a man to be fortunate as well as wise and just."

The period after Camden was perhaps the lowest point for the Patriot cause. Continental currency was all but worthless, there were mutinies in regiments of the Continental Army, and in September 1780, only a month after he had taken command of West Point, came Benedict Arnold's treason.

Arnold had turned traitor months before, having opened communication with the British when he was in command in Philadelphia, then sought a command where he could be of the most use to his new masters. Convincing Washington to give him the West Point assignment, Arnold immediately opened negotiations with the British to surrender that post along with Washington during an inspection trip there.

The plot was discovered quite by chance on the morning of September 23 by some militiamen who had stopped a man they believed to be a suspicious civilian. That individual turned out to be British Major John André, the liaison between Arnold and Clinton. Letters discovered in his shoe proved André's undoing. Informed of the arrest of one John Anderson, the name that André was using, Arnold immediately fled to the protection of a British warship in the Hudson.

Greene learned of Arnold's treason in a letter from Colonel Alexander Hamilton of Washington's staff on the evening of September 25. He immediately rushed two regiments to West Point to reinforce its garrison and ordered the army to be ready to march on short notice if Clinton moved. Washington, returning from his meeting at Hartford, arrived at West Point just after Arnold had fled.

Washington ordered André sent under guard to Greene at Tappan and appointed a court of fourteen officers to try him. Greene was its president. The court convened on September 29 and rendered a unanimous verdict that André was a spy. The next day Washington decided that André was to be executed on October 1. A letter to that effect was sent to Clinton in New York. According to the Americans, André's only hope was an exchange for Arnold, which Clinton rejected, although the British commander did appeal that his aide's life be spared. Colonel Beverly Robinson, Clinton's personal representative, met with Greene at Sneden's Landing opposite Dobbs Ferry on October 1, offering to exchange anyone in British custody for André, but Washington only wanted Arnold. The next day, Greene paraded the army to witness the execution. André met his death bravely. Washington rejected André's request that he be allowed a soldier's death by firing squad, but he did allow André the concession of wearing his uniform. André was executed on October 2. He placed the rope around his neck himself.

Gates's defeat and Arnold's treason opened new possibilities for Greene. With Pickering having mastered the procedures, Greene at last gave up the post of quartermaster general. Now without specific assignment, he clearly wanted the southern command. This prospect horrified Caty and his brother Jacob, who wrote Greene on October 1, 1780: "She [Caty] is much Alarmed for fear you Should go to the Southward. You will Do well to Satisfy her of this Matter if you are not going which I wish you may not as Nothing but Disgrace and Disappointment had [has] Attended Every Commander on that Station."

It is clear in a letter Greene wrote to his friend in Congress John Mathews of South Carolina on October 3, 1780, that he wanted the appointment: "It is not my wish that the unfortunate should be sacrificed to vulgar prejudices, but if you find it necessary to appoint another officer to that [Southern] command, and think I can be useful in that quarter, my best endeavors will not be wanting to protect the people and serve my Country."

When he believed that Gates would continue in command, Greene wrote Washington on October 5 to request Arnold's former command of West Point instead. Washington immediately agreed, appointing Greene to the post the next day. He assigned Greene four brigades and ordered him to move them to West Point as rapidly as possible. On arrival, he was to move to put the works in "the most perfect state of defense." Washington told Greene that he had "full confidence in your prudence vigilance activity and good conduct."

Greene was not fated to remain at West Point for long. Congress had taken up the matter of the Camden disaster. Not only did it decide to look into Gates's handling of the battle, but there arose a demand that Greene be appointed in Gates's stead. Within a week of Greene's having assumed command at West Point, Knox wrote him that Gates was indeed to be removed from his command, and that this time Congress would allow Washington to name his replacement. "Who will that person be? You may ask me the same question, but I protest I know not."

Greene's performance in the recent fighting in New Jersey, especially his effective use of the New Jersey militia, impressed some members of Congress and apparently caused them to endorse his appointment to command in a region where militia were a far more important component of the armed forces than in the North. Washington was delighted when on October 14, barely a week after the West Point appointment, Congress gave him the authority to name a new commander in the South. He wrote Greene the same day. It is one of the few letters from Washington to one of his general officers in his own hand: "As Congress have been pleased to leave the Officer to command on this occasion to my choice, it is my wish to appoint you. And from the pressing situation of affairs in that quarter, of which you are not unapprised, that you should arrive there, as soon as circumstances will possibly admit." After only that of the commander in chief, Greene's new command was certainly the most important in the army.

On October 22, Washington told Greene that he had full confidence in him and would not presume to tell him how to conduct his affairs: "Uninformed as I am of the enemy's force in that quarter, of our own, or of the resources which it will be in our power to command for carrying on the War, I can give you no particular instructions but must leave you to govern yourself intirely according to your own prudence and judgement and the circumstances in which you find yourself."

On October 16, Greene requested a brief leave to return home to Rhode Island. His youngest child, Nathanael Ray, was recovering from a serious illness. He also knew that Caty would certainly be upset about his assignment in the South, and he wanted time to mollify her. Greene wrote Washington: "I will prepare myself for the command as soon as I can. But as I have been five years and upwards in service . . . if it was possible I should be glad to spend a few days at home before I set out to the Southward; especially as it is altogether uncertain how long my command may continue. . . ." Washington believed the situation in the South was dire, and he denied the request: "I wish circumstances could be made to correspond with your wishes . . . but your presence with your command as soon as possible is indispensable."

The same day he wrote to Washington, Greene wrote to Caty, then on her way from Rhode Island to join him at West Point. Addressing her as "My Dear Angel," Greene expressed false disappointment at the news of his new posting: "What I have been dreading has come to pass. His Excellency General Washington by order of Congress has appointed me to the command of the Southern Army. . . . This is so foreign from my wishes that I am distressed exceedingly. . . ." These sentiments were quite untrue and most certainly were prompted by a heartrending letter he had just received from Caty.

As it turned out, Greene did not even have time for a farewell. He and Caty missed a planned rendezvous at Fishkill on the Hudson. She followed him as far as Philadelphia, then returned to Rhode Island.

Greene and Steuben, his second-in-command in the South, arrived in Philadelphia on October 27, there to plead for the resources to rebuild the Southern Army. They spent a week in the capital, but without successful result. Greene informed Washington, "Congress can furnish no money, and the Board of War neither clothing or other necessities. Indeed the prospect is dismal, and truly distressing. I beg your Excellency to urge unceasingly the necessity of forwarding supplies for the southern Army, as it will be impossible to carry on a winters campaign without clothing."

As he traveled south, Greene met with political leaders in Delaware, Maryland, and Virginia. While they pledged support, no material aid was forthcoming. Received by Martha Washington at Mount Vernon, Greene wrote the commander in chief regarding his talks with leaders in Maryland: "They promise me all the assistance in their power; but are candid enough to tell me, that I must place little dependance upon them, as they have neither money or credit, and from the temper of the people are afraid to push matters to extremities." Virginia, expected to provide 3,500 men for the Continental Army, furnished only 1,500; and Governor Thomas Jefferson had promised one hundred wagons but furnished only eighteen. From Richmond, Greene wrote Washington in a reflective frame of mind:

> I cannot contemplate my own situation without the greatest degree of anxiety. I am far removed from almost all my friends and connections, and have to prosecute a war . . . attended with almost insurmountable difficulties, but doubly so now from the state of our finances and the loss of public credit. How I shall be able to support myself under all these embarrassments God only knows. My only consolation is, that if I fail I hope it will not be accompanied with any peculiar marks of personal disgrace. Censure and reproach ever follow the unfortunate. This I expect if I don't succeed; and it is only in the degree not in the entire freedom that I console myself. The ruin of my family is what hangs

most heavy upon my mind. My fortune is small; and misfortune or disgrace to me, must be ruin to them.

Greene arrived at the American camps at Charlottetown (Charlotte), North Carolina, on December 2. He was most gracious toward his disgraced predecessor, and Gates never forgot this courtesy and now became Greene's friend. The campaign in the South would pit against one another two of the most capable generals of the entire war. Greene and Corwallis each respected the other. The aggressive Cornwallis, now a lieutenant general at age forty-two, was arguably the best of the senior British generals in the war. He wrote of his new opponent: "Greene is as dangerous as Washington. He is vigilant, enterprising, and full of resources—there is but little hope of gaining any advantage over him. I never feel secure when encamped in his neighbourhood."

The situation appeared dire. South Carolina was virtually all in British hands; the members of the legislature were in hiding, and Governor John Rutledge had fled to North Carolina, which was in little better shape. Throughout the Carolinas there was bitter fighting between Patriots and Loyalists.

But British policy worked at cross-purposes, for the British sought to use the slave population in the South to destabilize the region by offering protection to those who escaped from their masters. Ironically this caused members of the Loyalist planter class to unite against the British. The British also shifted to a "pacification" strategy in which they planned to "Americanize" the war by turning over more of the fighting to the Loyalists. Their plan called for sending in a force of regulars in sufficient numbers to subdue an area. They would encourage Loyalists to rise up, then would arm them and have them hold the area. The problem with this was that the Loyalists who rallied to the British tended to be new, poor immigrants, and there was deep antagonism between them and the established classes. While the British hoped their new strategy would bring the reestablishment of royal authority, it ended up igniting a veritable civil war in which both sides were guilty of significant atrocities.

One significant Patriot success occurred after the Battle of Camden and before Greene's arrival. This was the Battle of King's Mountain on October 7, 1780. Some thirty miles west of Charlotte, it was an all-American Battle of Tory against Patriot. The Tory commander Major Patrick Ferguson was the only British officer present. While capable, Ferguson was also contemptuous of colonials and allowed his force to be surrounded at King's Mountain and there annihilated. Of Ferguson's 1,125 men, 1,105 were killed or captured. Ferguson was among the dead, having refused to surrender. Patriot losses were only 40 killed. This significant British defeat temporarily halted Cornwallis's efforts to secure North Carolina, but it had several negatives for Greene in that it seemed to end the immediate need to strengthen Patriot forces in the South and reinforced the belief held by some that militia alone could produce victory.

In his new command, Greene was blessed with able associates. Like Washington, one of his strengths was his willingness to value competence and to listen and learn from able subordinates. Greene especially relied on the brilliant tactician Brigadier General Daniel "Fighting Dan" Morgan, whose riflemen had played a key role in the Saratoga battles. Repeatedly passed over for promotion to brigadier general, Morgan had left the army in 1779, but patriotism motivated his return following the disaster at Camden, and he had been rewarded with promotion to brigadier general that October. Greene had known Morgan for some years, liked him a great deal, and sent for him immediately to be his second-in-command. Greene also relied heavily on two proven guerrilla leaders: former Continental Army lieutenant colonel and now brigadier general of South Carolina militia, Francis Marion, known as "the Swamp Fox"; and former Continental Army colonel, now South Carolina militia brigadier general, Thomas Sumter, "the Gamecock." Because of the small numbers of Continental Army regulars in the South, militia played a greater role. Although he had often disparaged the militia in the past, Greene now had to work with them, and he did all that he could to reach out to the militias and create an effective working relationship with their commanders.

Greene also relied heavily on the services of Colonel Thaddeus Kosciuszko of Poland, a close friend of Gates and chief engineer in the South. Brigadier General Isaac Huger from South Carolina was another capable senior officer. Cavalry was of immense importance in the southern campaign for reconnaissance but also for screening purposes, and Greene was fortunate in having a daring and effective commander in Lieutenant Colonel Henry "Light Horse Harry" Lee. Greene had met Lee at Brandywine, and the Virginian had served under him at Germantown. On Greene's petition to the commander in chief, Washington agreed to send Lee and his 280-man legion as part of Greene's command. Lee's Legion did not arrive in camp until January 8, 1781, however.

Colonel William Washington, a cousin of the army's commander in chief, was another able cavalrymen. Other key officers included Brigadier General Andrew Pickens and Colonel Otho Williams, who became Greene's adjutant general. Steuben, detached by Washington to train the Southern Army, was busy recruiting in Virginia. As his own quartermaster general, Greene selected able Lieutenant Colonel Edward Carrington, while the equally efficient

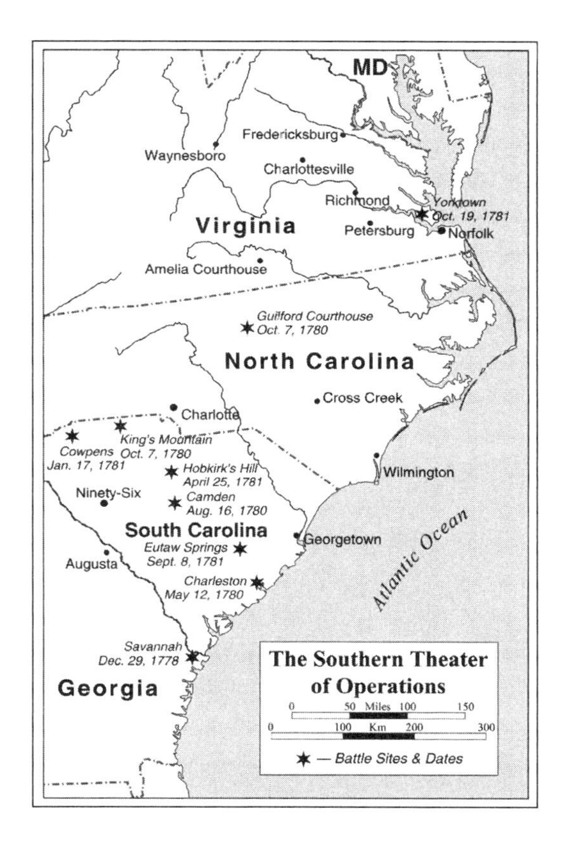

twenty-four-year-old Lieutenant Colonel William R. Davie became head of the Commissary Department. These were two excellent appointments. Despite able assistants, Greene would need all his organizational skills, his experience as quartermaster general, and his abilities as logistician.

On arrival at Charlotte on December 2, Greene immediately took a survey of his forces. He found that he had only 2,307 men, with 1,482 present for duty and only 800 of these sufficiently well-equipped to fight. The army had provisions for only a few days, and even clothing was in short supply. The supply situation was also far more critical than in the North. Greene summed up the situation in a letter to Washington: "Nothing can be more wretched and distressing than the condition of the troops, starving with cold and hunger, without tents and camp equipage. Those of the Virginia line are literally naked, and a great part unfit for any kind of duty, and must remain so untill clothing can be had from the Northward."

Physical conditions in the South were daunting. There were far fewer roads than in the North, and those existing were in poor repair. Much of the land was swamp, and transportation depended in large part on rivers, often difficult to navigate. Such conditions, however, favored the guerrilla warfare that was at first Greene's only possible recourse. Because there were so many rivers in the region, Greene recognized the important role that boats would play in the southern fighting, for resupply, but also for the movement forward and the extraction of his troops, should this prove necessary. Toward that end, he ordered as many boats collected as possible and even designed a shallow-draft craft capable of carrying fifty barrels of goods. Greene also immediately dispatched men to survey the rivers and report back with the important necessary information on depths, crossing points, and currents.

Cornwallis commanded some 3,224 veteran troops and outnumbered Greene in effective combat strength 4 to 1. Necessity forced Greene into a dramatic change of strategy. He now divided his army. Such a step, he knew, violated the basic military principle of concentration of force, but he believed he had no other choice. He would split his army into small guerrilla bands, yield territory, and wait for the right opportunity, while he rebuilt his strength and trained and equipped new recruits. Meanwhile, he planned to harass the British and inflict as many casualties as possible. Toward that end, Greene made special use of the rifle, exacting a growing tally of British casualties from long-range sniping fire.

Greene immediately dispatched Kosciuszko to find a more suitable location for the army to camp than Charlotte, the low ground of which made it more susceptible to disease and which was difficult to defend. Kosciuszko soon reported a favorable location in the Cheraw Hills near Cheraw, South Carolina, on the Pee Dee River. One of the few highlands of the Carolinas, it offered both a healthier location for the men and excellent forage for the horses. It was seventy miles distant from Cornwallis's principal camp at Winnsboro, where Cornwallis had moved after the Battle of King's Mountain. Another chief advantage of the Cheraw Hills location was that it prevented Cornwallis from establishing control of Crook Creek, which Greene believed would have given him command of the greatest part of the provisions of "the lower country." Greene approved of Kosciuszko's choice, and the army soon was established at Hick's Creek near Cheraw.

Greene informed Washington of his plans on October 31. He told the commanding general that he planned to field a force of about 1,000 infantry and 800 cavalry, supplemented by local militia forces, and to conduct partisan warfare. Greene reported, "I see but little prospect of getting a force to contend with the enemy upon equal grounds and therefore must make the most of a kind of partizan war untill we can levy and equip a larger force." Washington understood the necessity, replying to Greene on November 8, "I intirely approve of your plans for forming a flying Army."

Cornwallis remained confident that he could protect the forts that he had established in the interior. These included Camden to the southeast, Ninety Six to the southwest on the headwaters of the Saluda River, and Fort Granby to his south at the confluence of the Saluda and Congaree Rivers. Other British forts south of Winnsboro included Fort Motte at the junction of the Wateree and the Congaree, Fort Watson on the Santee, and Orangeburg on the Edisto. On the coast he held both Georgetown and Charleston (where he had a large garrison), and he had the advantage of rich farmlands to his rear, from which he could provision his troops.

CHAPTER EIGHT

GREENE'S SOUTHERN CAMPAIGN: FIRST PHASE

GREENE'S DECISION OF DECEMBER 16, 1780, TO DIVIDE HIS army was one of the most important of the entire war. Interestingly, unlike Washington, he decided this entirely on his own without calling a council of war to ask the advice of his subordinates. Greene's plan violated every principle of war, which called for an army to concentrate against a stronger foe. Dividing the army appeared to allow the British the opportunity to destroy the scattered parts piecemeal.

Before moving his headquarters from Charlotte to the Cheraw Highlands, Greene sent Morgan and 300 of his best troops, along with Colonel Washington's light dragoons—about 600 men in all—to the southwest to take up position on the Pacolet River in western South Carolina on Cornwallis's left flank. Morgan established a position some 140 miles from Greene's own, between the Pacolet and the Broad Rivers. There he would be joined by 300 volunteers and up to 400 South Carolina and Georgia militiamen. Morgan was now in position to threaten British posts at both Ninety Six and Augusta, but Greene's decision was risky, for the two major units of his army were too far apart to be mutually supporting.

Logistics played an important role in the decision. Dividing the army had the great advantage of making it easier to feed and supply. Greene also expected Morgan to buoy Patriot morale in the western country of South Carolina, but he did not believe Morgan would be able to accomplish much offensively. Greene wrote Lafayette that Morgan's men, especially with the British being reinforced, were simply too few in number to make any "opposition of consequence."

Greene, meanwhile, moved the bulk of his force, 1,100 men, 650 of whom were Continentals, from Charlotte, arriving at his new camp on December 26, 1780. He was well pleased with Kosciuszko's arrangements. The Pole had laid out an excellent and well-defended camp.

Lee's Legion arrived several weeks later, and Greene detached it to support Lieutenant Colonel Francis Marion's operations in South Carolina. Greene's moves had the effect of forcing Cornwallis to follow suit, for if the British concentrated for an attack on Greene, it would enable Morgan to move against and take Ninety Six or Augusta or both. Greene, however, could not hope to hold the territory below the falls of the Pee Dee River, for there were no defensible passes in that area. Roads were few, rivers were deep, and there were numerous swamps.

The immediate period after his move to Hick's Creek was a difficult one for Greene, who had to contend with many problems. Supply remained a cruel problem, and Greene despaired of carrying on the war with only militia. In mid-January 1781, he wrote Washington that what was needed in the South was "a good Army well appointed and supplied" of 4,000–5,000 infantry and

800–1,000 cavalry: "We have but a very little force in the field, and two thirds of them are totally unfit for duty; and unless clothing arrives soon I must disband them. I am persuaded unless the States have it in their power to levy[,] equip and support such an Army as I have mentioned these States are inevitably lost."

Apart from trying to secure adequate supplies, Greene spent his time training his men. He encountered numerous problems with the militia, especially in their comings and goings as they pleased. This was not a situation that the stern disciplinarian Greene, or any army commander for that matter, could tolerate. Greene issued orders that the next man who deserted would be hanged. When the inevitable happened, Greene had the deserter tried. Found guilty, he was hanged before the entire army. This unfortunate but necessary step ended the problem of desertions. As his men learned that he was a strict disciplinarian, they came to respect Greene for the fact that he was genuinely concerned about their welfare and willing to share their trials and discomforts.

British mounted forces meanwhile successfully employed irregular tactics and achieved tactical mobility equal or superior to that of the Continental forces. Twenty-six-year-old Lieutenant Colonel Banastre Tarleton, known as the "Hunting Leopard," became the leading figure of the ensuing highly mobile British irregular warfare in the South. Tarleton's Legion (known as the Green Dragoons for their green uniforms) was a highly effective unit. Tarleton's Legion became the terror of the South, but in the end this worked to Patriot advantage, alarming the population and driving previously apathetic civilians to the Patriot side.

Still, the British never had anything approaching the often-held ten-to-one manpower ratio of pacifying troops over guerrillas necessary to put down the latter. Thus the British were never able to eliminate the irregulars entirely. With neither side able to protect its civilian supporters, a ferocious guerrilla war soon spread through South Carolina and into Georgia and North Carolina. Greene informed president of the Continental Congress Samuel Huntington, "The whole country is in danger of being laid waste by the Whigs [Patriots] and Torys [Tories], who pursue each other with as much relentless fury as beasts of prey."

In order to support Cornwallis and prevent reinforcement of Greene, General Clinton dispatched Benedict Arnold, now a brigadier general in the British Army, and 1,600 men to the Chesapeake to destroy the Southern Army's supply depots. Arnold moved with ruthless efficiency, forcing Virginia legislators to flee westward from the capital of Richmond and nearly taking Governor Jefferson prisoner. Steuben attempted to reorganize Patriot forces in Virginia until Washington was able to send Lafayette and a slightly smaller force to oppose Arnold. This situation was quite worrisome for Greene, as Virginia was a critical leg of his supply route north. If Arnold were to be successful, Greene's army might easily be caught between two British forces and destroyed.

Meanwhile, 1,500 British reinforcements under Major General Alexander Leslie arrived in the South. This infusion of manpower enabled Cornwallis, in any case displeased with the results of his dispersion tactics, to carry out offensive operations. He decided that his first target of the now-divided Continental Army in the South would be Morgan. In early January 1781, Cornwallis dispatched Tarleton with his legion and some other troops to number 1,100 men to round up Morgan. Once that had been accomplished, Cornwallis planned to move against Greene.

Tarleton eagerly accepted the assignment. He was confident of an easy success. After all, he was facing only some 600 poorly equipped Continentals and several hundred militia. Greene and Morgan both had excellent intelligence as to the British moves, and on January 13 a surprisingly confident Greene wrote his subordinate: "Col. Tarleton is said to be on his way to pay you a visit. I doubt not but he will have a decent reception and a proper dismission. And I am happy to find you have taken every possible precaution to avoid a surprise."

Morgan took up a defensive position at a place known as the Cowpens, located near the North Carolina border and south of the Broad River. The location was so named because it had been used for many years for grazing cattle. The Battle of Cowpens took place on the morning of January 17, 1781, and was a tactical masterpiece. Counting militia, Morgan may have had as many as 2,000 men, while Tarleton had 1,100. Knowing of Tarleton's approach, Morgan selected a hill as the center of his position. He arranged his forces so as to take advantage of their strengths, while at the same time concealing their weaknesses. The defenders were in three lines: riflemen in front, then militia, and finally the Continental Line. He ordered his riflemen to fire two rounds—they were to aim for the British officers—and then move to the rear as a reserve. The militiamen were to wait until the British were at point-blank range, then fire a volley and in turn move to the rear. Finally, there was the Continental Line, who would meet the British on the hill's crest, if need be with the bayonet. Morgan concealed his cavalry under William Washington behind the hill.

On locating Morgan, the impetuous and over-confident Tarleton forewent a reconnaissance in favor of an immediate attack and took the withdrawal of the first two Patriot ranks as the beginning of a rout. When Tarleton's men rushed the final rank of the Continental Line, Morgan ordered the cavalry to attack Tarleton's right flank. At the same time, the militia—having reformed—struck the British left. In this small-scale repeat of the Battle of Cannae of 216 B.C., Tarleton lost 90 percent of his force. He himself escaped along with some of his cavalry, but Tarleton left behind on the field 100 dead, 229 wounded, and 600 unwounded prisoners. Morgan's losses were only 12 killed and 60 wounded. More important for Morgan, he had secured some 800 muskets, 2 cannon, 100 horses, and all the British supplies and ammunition. Soon the British prisoners were headed north, guarded by Virginia militiamen whose term of enlistment had expired.

The Battle of Cowpens was a major disaster for the British. It completely transformed the situation in the South, which had seemed so close to a Patriot disaster just weeks before. Patriot morale now soared. But Morgan had in fact taken a considerable gamble, and his decision to fight was probably as mistaken as that of Gates, although fortunately it had a far different outcome for the Patriot cause.

Greene feared that this one victory might serve to convince those in the North that the South no longer needed supplies and aid. He summed up his concerns to his friend James Varnum: "This Army is in a deplorable condition; and not withstanding this little success, must inevitably fall a prey to the enemy if not better supported, than I see a prospect of. Dont imagine that Lord Cornwallis is ruined: for depend upon it, the Southern States must fall, unless there is established a well appointed Army for their support. . . ."

Greene was correct: the war in the South was far from over, and Morgan was in fact now in serious danger. Acutely aware of this, by the evening of January 17 Morgan had already withdrawn across the Broad River, headed for the Little Catawba River. Cornwallis was determined to pursue Morgan into North Carolina with his main army, but he probably thought that Morgan would not be so quick to move, and he waited for Leslie to come up in order to increase his numbers. Thus it was January 19 before Cornwallis was able to initiate the pursuit with about 2,500 men. Failing to catch Morgan at Ramseur's Mill, North Carolina, on January 25, Cornwallis there decided to convert all his troops to light infantry in order to speed his march, his actual light infantry under Tarleton having been lost at Cowpens. Cornwallis paused for two days, ordering his men to burn their excess wagons and baggage train, leaving only a few wagons for ammunition, medical supplies, and transport of wounded. He then set out again.

Morgan was having personal problems. Afflicted with a reccurrence of chronic sciatica, he could barely ride and so traveled part of the way by wagon. Both armies also had to deal with steady rain and deep mud. But when Cornwallis reached the Catawba River on January 30, he learned that Morgan had already crossed. The river was now swollen as a result of the heavy rains, and Cornwallis had no option but to pitch camp and wait for the water to recede.

Greene, meanwhile, had decided he must reunite with Morgan. He had contemplated a quick attack on Ninety Six in the hopes of drawing Cornwallis away from Morgan, but realized that this was not feasible as the enlistments of the Virginia militia would soon be up and because his own force was in poor condition. Instead, he would rendezvous with Morgan, withdraw north where his own supply lines into Virginia would be shorter and those of Cornwallis considerably longer, and then find the right moment to turn and strike his pursuers.

Greene ordered his own portion of the army to march toward Salisbury, North Carolina. Getting Morgan's force to safety was a priority, and with Morgan now in such poor health, Greene believed he should be there himself. Riding to Morgan was a considerable risk, for his route took Greene through a heavily Tory area, and he traveled with only one aide. It was also not an easy passage, for the roads were in terrible condition from the recent rain.

Greene reached Morgan's camp on the Catawba on January 30, the same day that Cornwallis was making his own camp on the other side of the river. Sensing an opportunity to defeat Cornwallis, Greene immediately wrote out orders summoning local militia in order to contest the crossing of the Catawba when the river went down, reasoning that he would have sufficient time for the men to assemble. The very day of Greene's arrival, however, the river began to recede, and by the next day it was apparent to Greene that he could not make a stand at that point. He then ordered Morgan to fall back on Salisbury, North Carolina, near the Yadkin River.

Cornwallis decided to try to cross the Catawba on the night of January 31–February 1. The river line was held by a rear guard of North Carolina militia under Brigadier General William Davidson, who had collected some 800 men and posted them to cover four likely crossing points along thirty miles of the river. The largest number, some 300 men, were at Beattie's Ford, beyond which lay Morgan's camp. Cornwallis, however, decided to try to outflank the Americans by crossing at another point and then getting in behind them. He ordered a demonstration against Beattie's Ford while he led the bulk of his men across the river at Cowan's (or McCowan's) Ford, six miles below it. At that location, the river was some five hundred yards wide and three to four feet deep with a swift-moving current.

With rain beginning again, Cornwallis knew the river would soon be up. In the distance he could see fires burning in the Patriot camp, and just before dawn on February 1, Cornwallis sent his men across at Cowan's Ford, the soldiers holding their muskets and cartridge boxes high above their heads as they waded through the chilly water. The American sentries spotted the British crossing and soon opened fire. Cornwallis's horse was shot underneath him, but managed to make the opposite shore before dying.

As Cornwallis soon learned, the campfires were a ruse. Morgan had departed the evening before. In the ensuing fighting, however, Davidson was slain, and the American rearguard militia, outlined by the light of their own campfires for the British, soon fled.

Greene had remained behind, hoping without great success to secure militia and then to rendezvous with Davidson's force. He had expected that the Battle of Cowpens would serve as a powerful recruiting tool, but in this was to be disappointed. As Greene explained in a letter to Samuel Huntington, "The people have been so harassed for eight months past and their domestick matters are in such distress that they will not leave home; and if they do it for so short a time that they are of no use."

With the militia now dispersed, Greene made his way north, stopping in a house near Tarrant's Tavern, halfway to Salisbury. From there he sent a messenger to Brigadier General Isaac Huger, commanding the main Continental force at Hick's Creek in his absence, to move the army and join Morgan's men at Salisbury as soon as possible. Greene planned to withdraw across the Dan River into Virginia. He had already issued orders to collect boats on the river to ferry the army across. Across the Dan he would be closer to supplies that he had ordered sent on ahead, as well as to anticipated reinforcements Steuben was gathering.

Learning of Davidson's death and the scattering of the militia, Greene was soon on his way in the rain, riding for Salisbury. He narrowly escaped capture by Tarleton's cavalry a few miles beyond

Tarrant's Tavern. Cornwallis was only a few hours behind with every expectation of this time trapping the Americans, but he did not know of the special shallow-draft boats. If he could reach the Yadkin in time, Morgan would be able to cross over, while Cornwallis could not.

Morgan arrived at the Yadkin on February 2. The river was swollen by the heavy rains, but the boats were there. The crossing was slowed by a number of townspeople from Salisbury who, learning that the British were in close pursuit, insisted on fleeing with the army. Still, most of Morgan's men and the townspeople managed to cross over before Cornwallis's advance guard reached the river on the morning of February 3. Cornwallis learned that Shallow Ford, ten miles up the river, was always fordable, and he headed for it. This movement away from Greene and Morgan seemed reasonable, because Cornwallis expected that the Dan would be up, and his spies had informed him that Morgan would not be able to get across with the boats available. Cornwallis thus fully expected to pin Morgan's force against the Dan and there destroy it. Then he would deal with the main American body under Greene, and, once it too had been disposed of, the war in the South would be pretty much over.

Huger was unable to reach Salisbury in time, and Greene changed the assembly point to the small town of Guilford Court House between the Dan and the Haw. On February 8, Greene and Morgan broke camp and headed for Guilford Court House. Lee's Legion had already joined Huger, and on February 9, Greene's entire army had come up. Greene now briefly debated giving battle to Cornwallis at Guilford Court House. The terrain favored the Americans, but the absence of significant numbers of militia decided the issue. Greene had only 2,036 men with 1,426 of these regulars and most newly enlisted. Cornwallis had twice Greene's strength where it counted, in regulars.

Greene had no other realistic option but to continue the withdrawal into Virginia, where he expected to be reinforced. This time, however, Greene held a council of war, meeting with Morgan, Huger, and Otho Williams, probably only to secure their support for a decision already taken that might be considered as damaging to his military reputation. His subordinates concurred that it would be foolish to risk the army and that the only viable alternative was to withdraw into Virginia. Greene wrote Washington on February 9, summarizing events thus far and informing him that he was abandoning North Carolina: "We have no provisions but what we receive from our daily collections. Under these circumstances I called a council who unanimously advised to avoid an action and to retire beyond the Roanoke [the Dan] immediately." As Greene put it to General Thomas Sumter that same day, "If I should risque a General action in our present situation, we stand ten chances to one of getting defeated, & if defeated all the Southern States m[ust] fall."

Greene would have to hurry if he was to beat Cornwallis to the Dan, however. The British were only thirty-five miles away and closing fast. The final leg of the race for the Dan began on February 10. Greene's chief concern was that Arnold in Virginia might somehow affect a juncture with Cornwallis. Washington, who was following events, no doubt with some anxiety, wrote Greene, "Amidst the complicated dangers with which you are surrounded, a confidence in your abilities is my only consolation."

Greene sent his wagons and all unnecessary equipment on ahead. Unknown to Cornwallis, Greene had already ordered collection of all boats, to be employed wherever he should decide.

But even with the boats, it would take time for Greene to cross. If he was to escape the British, it was essential to create a diversion to deceive Cornwallis as to the actual crossing point. Greene therefore divided his force, creating a 700-man light corps to act as the army's rear guard and harass the British. He had hoped Morgan could command it, but he was too ill and indeed soon left the army to recuperate. Command went to Otho Williams. His 700 men were handpicked, selected on the basis of being the most fit and best shots, as well as their loyalty to the cause. Lieutenant Colonel John Eager Howard of Maryland commanded the rear guard infantry of 280 Continentals. There were also 60 Virginia riflemen. The rear guard also included all of Greene's cavalry. Lee commanded the cavalry element, which included his own legion.

Greene began the march from Guilford to the Dan on February 10, one day after Morgan and Greene's forces had merged. Soon, British scouts reported to Cornwallis the presence of a large number of Continentals ahead—both infantry and cavalry—presumably heading for the Dan. Because of its size, Cornwallis assumed the rear guard was the entire Continental force, and he set out after it. This belief was strengthened by the fact that it appeared to be making for the fords on the narrower upper Dan, where Cornwallis assumed Greene would attempt to cross. Greene, however, had arranged for the boats to be waiting for the army further downstream, at Irwin's Ferry.

During the next several days, Cornwallis strained to catch up, moving at up to thirty miles a day—a tremendous feat, given the alternately frozen-at-night and muddy-by-day state of the roads. Gradually Williams drew Cornwallis off to the west, until his men and Greene's own column with the bulk of the exhausted men were actually moving north on two parallel but not widely separate tracks. Tight security was essential, for if Cornwallis were to discover the trick, he could possibly defeat the two American columns in detail.

The Americans suffered on the rapid march north. Shoes were worn out and blankets were in short supply. Few of the men got much sleep. Greene got even less, for he spent most of the nights writing appeals for assistance and making out reports. He seemed to be everywhere on the march north, and his men respected him for that, giving him every bit of their effort; however, many of the militiamen, worried about families left behind, deserted, and Greene gave up trying to stop them.

Greene instructed Williams that the two parts of the army not be separated by more than a few miles. This was in case he might have to recall Williams; he wanted him to be able to come up quickly. But Greene also feared that his plan might already have been compromised, confiding in Williams that he believed "one of Tarleton's officers was in our camp night before last."

Cornwallis was however, certain he was pursuing Greene's entire force and that he would soon be able to catch it. Brigadier General Charles O'Hara, an outstanding officer, had command of Cornwallis's advance force. For three days the pursuit continued, with O'Hara only hundreds of yards behind Lee's cavalry, which was protecting Williams's rear. To prevent a surprise night attack, Lee posted double guards. The infantrymen slept in turns; half remained awake, while the other stood guard. The cavalrymen patrolled at night, getting only six hours sleep out of every forty-eight. Meanwhile, Kosciuszko and Carrington had rounded up all watercraft along a thirty-mile stretch of the Dan. Kosciuszko had also supervised construction of strong earthworks on the north side of the river to make Cornwallis pay a prohibitive price if he tried to force a passage.

On the third day of the march, Tarleton, eager to engage the Americans, pushed forward and closed with Lee. A short, sharp fight ensued between the opposing cavalry units, in which Tarleton lost 18 men killed and Lee only 2. Tarleton then broke off the engagement. Although Tarleton made no further effort to close with Lee, the British advance and the American rear guard were certainly within sight of one another, and shots were frequently exchanged.

On the night of February 13, Williams's men could see the light of campfires on the horizon and assumed these to be the bivouac fires of Greene's army on the south side of the river, halted to stand and fight. Word spread that the men would soon have to engage a British force four times their own in size in order to give their compatriots the chance to escape. But word soon came down that the campfires were intended for Williams's men and that Greene's baggage was even then being sent across the river and the men would soon follow. A loud cheer went up from the Americans, heard by Cornwallis, who wondered at its meaning. At midnight the British were on the move again, and Williams was forced to hastily break camp.

The Dan was still forty miles from the campfires, and Cornwallis was determined to cover the distance in the next twenty-four hours. Williams, however, covered it in only sixteen hours. Hardly had the march resumed early on February 14 than a dispatch rider appeared and delivered a message from Greene: "The greater part of our wagons are over, and the troops are crossing." Williams informed the men, and they again cheered.

That evening another courier appeared with yet another dispatch from Greene at Irwin's Ferry, ten miles into Virginia: "½ past 5 o'clock. The troops are all across, the stage is clear." Greene pronounced himself ready to "receive" Williams and give him a "hearty welcome."

Once again, Williams's men cheered loudly when the news was passed to them. Three hours later when Tarleton's men reached the Dan, it was to find that the Americans were all safely across the river with no boats to be found on the south bank. Colonel Carrington, whose hard work had made the escape possible, crossed in the last boat with Lee. The broad, swift-flowing Dan allowed the Americans to get a good night's sleep for the first time since the march had begun. Greene informed Washington on February 15, "we have crossed without the loss of either men or Stores." Greene went on to note, however, the "miserable situation" facing his men for want of clothing and shoes, "several hundreds of the Soldiers tracking the ground with their bloody feet."

Greene's two-hundred-mile march from Cowpens, which included the crossing of four rivers, is today regarded as a minor military masterpiece, one of the great operations in American military history. Even Tarleton praised it. He wrote later, "Every measure of the Americans during their march to Virginia was judiciously designed and vigorously executed."

Cornwallis had failed to destroy Greene's army, but he did at least have the satisfaction of now holding North Carolina unopposed. With no means of crossing the Dan or of sustaining his army so distant from his own supply depots, however, on February 17 he withdrew his men south sixty miles to Hillsboro. There he issued a victory proclamation as an inducement to recruit militia in this heavily Loyalist area. The numbers of men who rallied to him were disappointing, however. Cornwallis wrote in a letter to Germain in London that men were reluctant to volunteer "while a doubt remained on their minds of the superiority of our Arms."

Cornwallis thus found himself caught between a rock and hard place. He was short of military supplies, and the nearest major British base was on the coast at Wilmington. A march there, however, would undoubtedly invite harassing attacks from Greene en route.

Greene was also disappointed, for the expected reinforcements in the form of Pennsylvania Continentals had been delayed and then diverted to Virginia. Confident they would appear in due time, Greene sought in the meantime to at least keep his opponent off-balance and to dissuade Loyalists from rallying to Cornwallis. On February 18, Greene sent Lee and his legion and Pickens with some Continental infantry back across the Dan to operate in conjunction with Patriot militia. Two days later he also dispatched Williams and the light infantry.

Until reinforcements and supplies, including ammunition, appeared, Greene's chief concern was that Lee and Pickens not overreach and allow themselves to be cut off and destroyed. To prevent that from happening, Greene crossed the Dan himself on February 22, riding eighteen miles south of the river to meet with Lee and Pickens. He caught a few hours sleep and then rode back to the army before daybreak. When this became known in the army, it added to the men's confidence in Greene's leadership.

While Greene was with Pickens and Lee, word arrived that Tarleton was operating in the vicinity. Assuming correctly that he had been detached to recruit Loyalists for the British forces, Greene ordered his subordinates to intercept and destroy the Green Dragoons. A trail of burned farmhouses guided the Americans, who nearly caught Tarleton dining at a farmhouse.

Lee's men wore green uniforms similar to those of Tarleton, and several Tory militia scouts mistook Lee for Tarleton and informed him that they were being followed by Colonel John Pyle and some 350 Loyalists on their way to join the British. Lee deceived the scouts, posing as Tarleton, and sent them back to Pyle with orders to draw his men up for inspection. Lee ordered Pickens to follow him and to conceal his militiamen in some woods, while he himself led his horsemen forward in single file with drawn sabers as if reviewing the militia. Lee planned that once he had the militia surrounded, he would demand their surrender. But before he could accomplish this, one of the Loyalists identified Pickens's men in the woods and fired his musket in alarm. Lee's men immediately wheeled and attacked the Loyalists, who had their rifles and muskets still slung. Within a span of ten minutes, 90 Loyalists were cut down in what came to be called "Pyle's Massacre." Most of the remainder were wounded, Pyle among them. Not a man on Lee's side was killed, and he lost only one horse. Lee did not order a pursuit. As might be expected, the engagement sharply curtailed Cornwallis's recruiting efforts.

Informed of events by some of Pyle's men who escaped, Tarleton sent out scouts, who located Lee's camp. Tarleton planned a night attack on the Americans but called it off when he received an order from Cornwallis, who had learned that Greene had been seen south of the Dan and, assuming he had his entire army with him, ordered Tarleton to rejoin the main body of the army. Cornwallis then broke camp on the Haw River, crossing over to the south side on February 27 and taking up a new position on the Alamance River, a tributary of the Haw, which becomes the Cape Fear River halfway to the coast at Wilmington. Cornwallis hoped to be able to compel Greene to fight when he would be at a numerical disadvantage.

Greene was already in motion. In late February, having finally received some 400 Continental recruits from Steuben in Virginia, along with 1,060 North Carolina and 1,693 Virginia militia, Greene took his army back across the Dan and established a position north of Cornwallis. He still did not believe his forces strong enough to engage Cornwallis in pitched battle, but he hoped that he might harass Cornwallis, interrupt his lines of communication, and intimidate the Tories of the region. This was a delicate business, however, for at the same time Greene had to prevent Cornwallis from slipping behind him, cutting his supply line to Virginia, and forcing him to fight at numerical disadvantage.

Three streams flow together to become the Haw. The Alamance is the southernmost, the northern branch is Troublesome Creek, and the central stream is Reedy Fork. Greene took up position between Troublesome Creek and Reedy Fork, just north of Cornwallis's own location. Greene hoped this position would allow him, if necessary, to withdraw north and cross the Dan again. Not wishing to remain in a fixed position so that Cornwallis could mount an attack, Greene changed his camp frequently, not remaining in any one area more than two nights. Presuming British spies to be about, he also did not divulge his planned movements until they were actually in progress.

Confident of his own now-proven sound military judgment, Greene kept his own counsel. He alone considered the options, then decided what he thought best for the circumstances. Greene appeared tireless. He was up at dawn and spent the days inspecting his men and attending to the needs of the army. He also continued his usual practice of writing reports and keeping up with correspondence late into the night, usually going to sleep after only taking off his boots.

In the meantime, Greene sent out scouts and Williams's light infantry to protect his main body and provide early warning of any major move in his direction by Cornwallis. Because Greene's forces seemed to be constantly on the move, area Loyalists never knew where he would appear, and as a result, few joined Cornwallis. At the same time, Greene's men tangled with British foraging parties, making it difficult for Cornwallis to secure food.

Meanwhile, all of Cornwallis's efforts to snap up Greene's screening forces were unsuccessful, foiled by alert American scouts. On March 2, Lee's Legion and Virginia militia under Colonel William Preston clashed with Tarleton and inflicted losses on the British. Four days later, on March 6, the largest of these skirmishes occurred at Wetzel's Mills on Reedy Fork, in which Pickens's command fought with the British advance.

Greene now had some 4,000 men, a force large enough, he believed, to be able to challenge Cornwallis in the field. He intended to strike a blow while he enjoyed numerical advantage over his opponent and before the militia enlistments were up and they went home. On March 10, Greene dissolved Williams's independent command and absorbed these men back into the main army. He then moved to Guilford Court House, where he expected to do battle with Cornwallis.

Indeed, both sides now sought battle. Cornwallis, too, was eager for a showdown. He was fast running short of military supplies, including ammunition, and was a considerable distance from his Wilmington base. His army was also short of food, which was becoming difficult to secure and was too often recaptured by raiding Patriot forces. Worse for Cornwallis, the number of British desertions was rising, for the privations of the winter of 1781 had taken a heavy toll on morale. Far from his own home, the average British soldier did not feel the personal motivation felt by the Americans. Many of Greene's men believed they were fighting for "liberty," while many others fought for the security of their very homes. Desertions to Greene included some members of the elite British Guards. One decisive victory, Cornwallis reasoned, would restore morale, not only with the Loyalists, but among his own troops as well.

The pressure was not as great on Greene, but there was some criticism in the North of his constant maneuvering and refusal to engage the British in pitched battle. On March 10, 1781, Greene wrote Jefferson, stating that he was well aware of this sentiment, but noting the absence of promised reinforcements and the unreliable nature of the militia. He was, he said, confident in his own tactics: "Let the consequences of Censure be what it may, nothing shall hurry me into a Measure that is not Suggested by prudence or connects with it the interest of the department in which I have the honor to command."

Greene was not one to be swayed by outside pressures. He knew the true situation on the ground far better than any of his distant critics. The battle would occur only when he judged the time to be right, but he knew that even a modest success might produce sufficient numbers of British casualties to force Cornwallis to withdraw to Wilmington, harassed by Greene's forces. Greene subsequently justified the Battle of Guilford Court House to Washington in these words: "The difficulty of subsisting Men in this exhausted Country, together with the great advantages which would result from the action, if we were victorious, and the little injury if we were otherwise, determin'd me to bring on an action as soon as possible."

CHAPTER NINE

GUILFORD COURT HOUSE

THE OPPOSING SOUTHERN ARMIES AT LAST JOINED BATTLE at Guilford Court House on March 15, 1781. It was one of the more important battles of the war. On paper, Greene had the superior force: 4,404 men, including 4,243 infantry and 161 cavalry. This numerical advantage was deceptive, however, for only a third of this force, 1,490 men, consisted of Continental troops, and only about 500 of them—a regiment from Maryland, a company from Delaware, and the foot soldiers of Lee's Legion—could be judged trained veterans. The great majority of Greene's men were unreliable militia. Greene had no confidence in militia standing against British regulars, but he could hope that they would each be able to fire two or three rounds before fleeing the battlefield and that the Continentals would get the job done. Cornwallis had only 1,900 regulars, but almost all were disciplined veterans, steady under fire.

Greene had earlier reconnoitered the area, and he now chose a battlefield position in sparsely settled country just west of Guilford Court House. Greene ordered his men to break camp at Speedwell Iron Works on the morning of March 14. They then marched the ten miles to Guilford Court House, arriving there on the afternoon of March 14. Cornwallis was a little more than ten miles to the southwest.

Greene expected a British attack the next day, moving up New Garden Road. Toward that end, he planned to defend a stretch of gradually rising terrain astride the road, forcing the British to attack him uphill. He would now employ the same tactic that had worked so well for Morgan at the Battle of Cowpens: positioning his forces in three ranks, the militia in front. The disadvantage at Guilford Court House was that the forest would make it impossible for Greene to see the first two ranks from his command position at the third.

About a half mile west of Guilford Court House, Little Horseshoe Creek flowed in a more or less north-south direction. East of it lay open fields, denuded of corn, and behind these were a rail fence and woods. Behind the fence line, Greene placed his least trained men: 1,000 North Carolina militia. Greene later told them that he expected each man to fire off two rounds at the advancing British before falling back. At worst, he expected this to create some British casualties. At best, it might even break up some formations.

The second rank, about three hundred to four hundred yards farther back and in the woods, consisted of Virginia militia. Greene reasoned that the trees would both provide cover for the defenders and also help break up the tight British formations. To stiffen militia resolve, Greene mixed among them some Virginia Continentals. Aware that a showdown was approaching, Morgan had written Greene on February 20. Noting the large number of Patriot militia, he commented: "If they fight you'l beat Cornwallis[,] if not, he will beat you and perhaps cut your regulars to pieces, which will be losing all our hopes." Morgan suggested selecting seasoned veterans from among the militia ranks and placing them to the rear of the militia along with riflemen on the flanks with orders to "shoot down the first man that runs." Probably at Greene's instigation, Brigadier General Edward Stevens, who had been humiliated when his men ran away at the Battle of Camden, did just that, placing several dozen riflemen behind the main militia ranks with instructions to fire on any who bolted.

Beyond the woods and several fenced fields and at the top of a rise just before Guilford Court House and about four hundred yards behind the second line, Greene established his final position. It consisted of the 1,400-man Continental Line: two regiments from Maryland and two from Virginia. To get to this position the British would have to cross a small stream. This third line was just to the west of north-south Reedy Fork Road and Guilford Court House itself.

Finally, Greene placed covering forces in the woods to each side of his lines. Lee's Legion was on the left flank. Colonel William Washington's dragoons and Colonel Charles Lynch's riflemen held the right.

There was no reserve. Well-aware of the stakes involved, Greene had no intention, if he could prevent it, of placing his army in jeopardy. If prudence required, the men would withdraw north up Reedy Fork Road to Salisbury.

The night of March 14–15 was cold with a light frost, but the day dawned bright and clear. Early in the morning, even before first light, a courier arrived from Lee, scouting off to the south, with news that Cornwallis was indeed on the move toward Greene's position. Toward noon, Greene's men could hear distant shots from a brief skirmish between Lee's troopers and Tarleton's mounted force.

Cornwallis arrived on the battlefield shortly after noon and immediately formed a line on both sides of the road with no reserve, a move demonstrating contempt for his opponent. Leslie's brigade was on the right. It consisted of the 71st British Regiment of Highlanders, a Hessian regiment, and the 1st Guards Battalion. On the left was Lieutenant Colonel James Webster's brigade of the 23rd and 33rd Regiments of Foot, the Grenadiers, and a second Guards battalion. In the woods to the British left, Cornwallis posted German jagers, armed with short-barreled, large-bore rifles, and the light infantry of the guards. Tarleton's mounted men, ordered not to move save on Cornwallis's express command, stood ready as an exploitive force.

The battle opened almost immediately. The Americans began it with artillery fire, and the British replied. Following a twenty-minute cannonade with little damage inflicted by either side, Cornwallis ordered his infantry forward. The British troops, no doubt still tired from their march to the battlefield, crossed Little Horseshoe Creek at about 1 p.m., then formed up in tight ranks and began advancing across the open field in front of them. Too soon, with the British still about 150 yards or so from the fence line, the North Carolina militia opened a ragged fire. Although dozens of British soldiers fell, the vast majority continued on.

At about fifty yards, the British halted and delivered a volley of their own before charging with the bayonet. The North Carolina militiamen promptly fled into the woods, many simply throwing

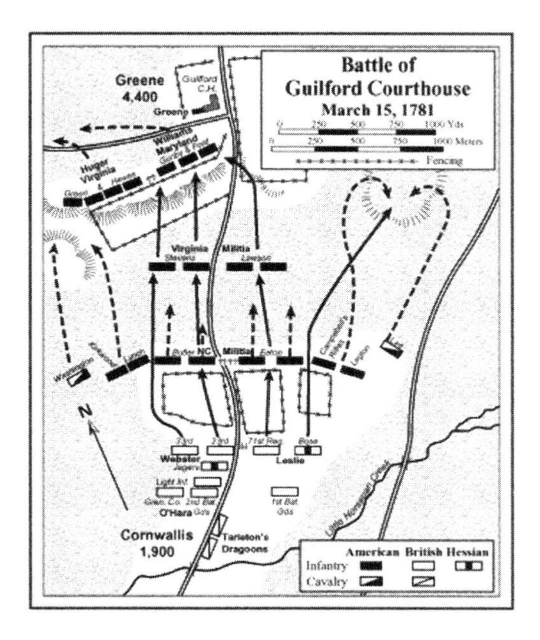

down their weapons as they attempted to escape, the British following. Unfortunately for Greene, most of the militia did not join their comrades-in-arms, the Virginians, but simply departed the battlefield altogether.

As Greene had anticipated, the woods broke up the British formations, and the battle became fragmented, with small groups of men engaging one another. Meanwhile on the British right flank, Cornwallis's Hessian regiment pursued the riflemen under Colonel William Campbell to a wooded hill about a half mile off to the southeast and were thus virtually removed from the main battle. In the main fight, the Virginia militia gave a good account of themselves, especially the men of Stevens's brigade, but, following about a half hour of fierce fighting and several bayonet attacks, and with Stevens wounded in the thigh, the British finally broke through the second American line and emerged from the woods, only to encounter an open fenced field and the third American line.

Greene had arranged his final line with Huger's two regiments of Virginians on the right and Williams's two Maryland regiments on the left. Lieutenant Colonel James Webster's men were the first British soldiers to emerge from the woods. They immediately moved across the field and up the rise toward the Continentals. A well-aimed volley and an American counterattack with the bayonet drove the British back and into the woods again. Webster was among the British casualties, mortally wounded.

This was the critical point in the battle, and Greene knew it. He might have ordered the Continental Line forward, but this chance at total victory would also carry with it the risk of the destruction of his entire army, something he was not prepared to hazard. He ordered the Continentals to hold their positions, and the British left was thus able to regroup.

Greene, meanwhile, rode up and down the American line, encouraging his men and in the process exposing himself to British fire. It appeared as if the Americans might carry the day, but on the British right/American left, things were going differently. Here the British 2nd Battalion of Guards managed to break through the 5th Maryland Regiment, a unit experiencing its first battle, and turned the American left. Many of the Marylanders fled without firing a shot, and disaster was averted only when Lieutenant Colonel John Eager Howard's 1st Maryland Regiment wheeled and hit the advancing British in the flank, and Colonel William Washington rode forward with his cavalry to strike the British from the rear.

To halt the American advance and stave off possible disaster, Cornwallis, whose horse had been shot from under him and who had only narrowly escaped capture, now ordered his artillery to fire grapeshot into the melee. This action killed as many British troops as it did Americans, but it also had the intended effect of breaking up the American counterattack that might well have decided the battle. The outcome was still in doubt, but Greene refused to hazard his army. The gap in his line convinced him he should order a retreat and preserve the bulk of his force. With most of the teams killed before the retreat began, the Americans now had to abandon their guns and two ammunition wagons. The men then moved north through the woods and up Reedy Creek Road, Howard's Marylanders providing rearguard protection for the withdrawing army.

Although the British initially pursued the Americans, they soon gave it up and rested at Guilford Court House. Greene set up his camp and defenses at his former location at the Speedwell Iron Works on Troublesome Creek. The next day, under flag of truce, both sides cared for their wounded and buried the dead.

In the battle the Americans had sustained 264 casualties: 79 killed and 185 wounded, more than half of them militia. Another 294 militia were listed as missing. They had simply deserted and returned home. British casualties in the battle were much higher: 93 killed and 439 wounded, a number mortally. This amounted to a quarter of the force engaged. Cornwallis reported a victory in glowing terms, but when Germain announced it to Parliament, opposition leader Charles James Fox responded by paraphrasing ancient King Pyrrhus of Epirus, "Another such victory would ruin the British Army." Horace Walpole gave an even gloomier assessment, saying that the battle showed that the war was lost. In his own report to Congress of March 16, Greene estimated British losses a bit high, at 600 men, but his assessment of the battle in a note to Washington a day later was realistic: "The honor of the Day terminated in favour of the Enemy, but their loss being infinitely greater than ours, I trust will ultimately prove advantageous to us."

Cornwallis remained at Guilford Court House for two days. This was Loyalist country, but few supplies were locally available for such a large force, and foraging parties would likely encounter Lee's Legion. Cornwallis thus reluctantly concluded, as Greene had hoped would be the case, that he had no recourse but to abandon the interior and march to Wilmington. He broke camp on March 18, leaving behind seventy British wounded under a flag of truce to be cared for by the Americans.

Greene followed, intent on harassing the British on their march. Greene would have to strike quickly if he were to have a chance, for many of the militia enlistments would be up at the end of March, and the men had made it clear they had no intention of remaining beyond their obligation. But on reaching Ramsey's Mills on the Haw River, the Americans found that Cornwallis had departed the night before for Cross Creek on the Cape Fear River. Cornwallis had hoped that there he might gather sufficient Tory recruits and supplies to resume the contest with Greene, but he was to be disappointed. He had no recourse but to continue to march his weary, half-starved army to Wilmington down the Cape Fear, which he reached on April 7. Meanwhile, Cornwallis informed his second-in-command, Lieutenant Colonel Rawdon, that he was to take over management of the war in South Carolina, protect its important British posts, and counter any attacks by Greene, which would now surely come.

At Wilmington, Cornwallis was able to replenish his supplies, thanks to the Royal Navy. This accomplished, he moved north into Virginia. Cornwallis was clearly frustrated by Greene's brand of war, writing that he was "quite tired of marching about the country in quest of adventures." Cornwallis hoped that in Virginia he could join Arnold's 2,500 British troops, already employing that state's east-west waterways to ravage the local economy, and cut the Patriot supply line to Greene in the South. Cornwallis departed Wilmington on April 24 and arrived at Richmond on May 20. Ultimately, he ended up at the small tobacco port of Yorktown.

Despite his tactical defeat at Guilford Court House, Greene understood that the battle had dramatically changed the entire strategic situation in the South. With the exception of the British coastal enclave of Wilmington, Greene controlled North Carolina. In a daring move, he now planned to march south with his small force of about 1,200 Continentals and 250 militia to carry the war to South Carolina. Here the prizes were a number of British posts, especially Camden and Ninety Six, and perhaps even Charleston and Augusta.

The campaign would not be an easy one. As Greene wrote Washington on March 29: "The Manoeuvre will be critical and dangerous; and the troops exposed to every hardship." Once again expressing concern for his reputation, Greene concluded with: "I shall take every effort to avoid a misfortune; but necessity obliges me to commit myself to chance and I trust my friends will do justice to my reputation if any accident attends me."

British forces at Rawdon's disposal were not negligible, numbering some 8,000 men, which Cornwallis had reasoned would be sufficient to deal with Greene. But two-thirds of these were militia, and the need to garrison numerous outposts in South

Carolina and Georgia meant that Rawdon's field force would be limited to only about 1,500 men at his main base of Camden. Greene could thus hope to meet Rawdon on something approaching equal terms, especially with Sumter and Marion conducting guerrilla operations in the state. On April 6, 1781, Greene departed Ramsey's Mills with some 1,500 men for South Carolina and a direct confrontation with Rawdon.

CHAPTER TEN

HOBKIRK'S HILL

GREENE'S IMMEDIATE OBJECTIVE IN SOUTH CAROLINA WAS to drive the British from their outposts along the Santee and the Congaree Rivers. Marion and Sumter had been carrying out hit-and-run raids in South Carolina, and while Greene was confident of Marion, he was less certain of Sumter. The most important British posts in South Carolina were Camden on the Wateree River, both the farthest north and the largest British fort; Georgetown, located near the mouth of the Pee Dee River; Ninety Six, near the source of the Saluda River (and so named because it was ninety-six miles from the chief Cherokee Indian village of Keowee); Fort Watson, about sixty miles from both Charleston and Camden; Fort Granby; Fort Motte; and Orangeburg.

Greene hoped to defeat the isolated British garrisons in detail, but his strategy was indeed a daring one, for it ran the risk of letting Cornwallis get in behind him and attack him from the rear.

Greene was confident, however. He wrote Steuben, who was still in Virginia: "The boldness of the manoeuvre will make them [the British] think I have secret reasons which they cannot comprehend. If I can get supplies and secure a retreat I fear no bad consequences." Greene explained to North Carolina Colonel James Emmet on April 3, "Dont be surprised if my movements dont correspond with your Idea of military propriety. War is an intricate business, and people are often saved by ways and means they least look for or expect."

On April 7, Greene put his small force in motion toward Camden. Aware that no assistance would be forthcoming from Washington and frustrated in the response to his requests of the state governments of the region, he wrote to Sumter and requested that the militia commander join him with his men and whatever supplies he could secure. Although Sumter responded with assurances, he in effect ignored the orders. Greene, meanwhile, remained unaware that the "Gamecock" had no plans to join him.

As he was camped on Lynches River, Greene learned that "Light Horse" Harry Lee and Francis Marion had taken the small British post at Fort Watson. Earlier, on February 28, Sumter had tried and failed to take that same place. When it came Marion's turn, he had laid siege to the fort's stockade of pointed logs and then awaited the arrival of artillery. In the interim, one of his officers suggested building a tower and positioning men in it to pick off those inside the fort. This was done and indeed prevented the British from firing on the Americans working to dismantle the fort's walls. The fort surrendered on April 23.

Their main position of Camden was an excellent natural position for the British. The Wateree River was a mile to the south and southwest, and on the east lay Pine Tree Creek. The fort consisted of redoubts and a stockade. Although Sumter never appeared, Greene was determined to proceed, and on April 19 he took up position at Hobkirk's Hill, an east-west pine-covered ridge astride the main north-south road to Camden, there to await the arrival of his artillery. Hobkirk's Hill was about a mile and a half north of Camden and three miles south of the battlefield where Gates had suffered his humiliating defeat eight months before. Greene now commanded 1,551 men: some 1,200 Continentals, 250 militia, and fewer than 100 cavalrymen under Washington.

Greene had hoped to catch Rawdon by surprise, but his approach was revealed by Loyalists, and Rawdon was ready and waiting. Rawdon was only twenty-six years old, young indeed for such an important independent command, but he had proved himself in fighting in America since the beginning of the war, rising from lieutenant at Bunker Hill in 1775, to lieutenant colonel in 1778. Certainly Cornwallis had full confidence in his abilities. Learning of the strength of the British position, Greene had planned to use his superior numbers, augmented by those of Sumter when he arrived, to lay siege to the British. However, a deserting drummer of the Maryland line carried word to Rawdon that Sumter had not yet arrived, that the Continental artillery was absent, that there had been desertions, and that the Americans were short of food. This information strengthened Rawdon's resolve not to begin his first major command with a withdrawal. By arming every man capable of carrying a weapon, including the musicians, Rawdon put together a force of 900 men.

Hopeful of taking Greene by surprise, Rawdon ignored the direct approach to Hobkirk's Hill along the main north-south road. On the morning of April 25, as Greene's men were having breakfast, Rawdon came in from the southwest through thick

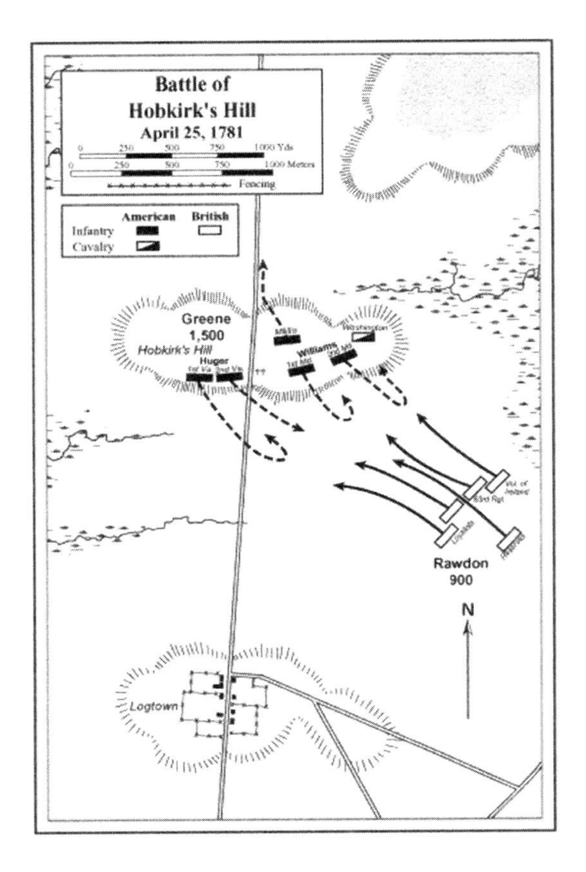

woods and on a narrow front. Unknown to the British, however, the American artillery had arrived.

Rawdon's men ran into Greene's pickets about 10 a.m. on April 25. Captain Robert Kirkwood led a spirited defense that purchased sufficient time for Greene to be able to deploy his forces, which were already largely in battle lines. Observing that the British were massed on a narrow front, Greene employed a more aggressive strategy than in his previous battles, deploying on a broad front so that he might be able to double envelop the attackers.

Greene's troops left their defensive positions on the hill and shifted off to the southeast. Williams's Marylanders held the American left, while Huger's Virginians were on the right. Washington's dragoons and some North Carolina infantry were in reserve to the left rear. Greene planned to have the 2nd Maryland Regiment strike the British right, while the 1st Virginia moved against the British left.

Rawdon attacked, but grapeshot from the American guns opened up a withering fire on the British ranks. Rawdon quickly realized Greene's intention and was able to bring up his own second echelon troops fast enough and deploy them in line to counter the Americans. Worse for Greene, Colonel John Gunby's 1st Maryland Regiment in the center of the American line performed poorly. Captain William Beatty, commanding its rightmost company, was killed early in the advance, and his men then halted in place. Rather than attempt to hurry the company forward, Gunby halted the entire regiment, then ordered it to march back to the base of the hill and reform. This movement exposed the flanks of regiments to either side, causing them to panic. Seeing this, Rawdon pressed the attack, his dragoons taking the three American guns. Greene was determined to save the guns, and he personally led a counterattack that helped to retrieve them, aided by a charge of Washington's cavalry that drove the British dragoons from the field. Greene then withdrew his men back to the crest of Hobkirk's Hill, Washington and Kirkwood holding the British dragoons at bay.

Greene expected and hoped that Rawdon would press the attack. He was convinced that his men, ashamed of their earlier withdrawal, would give a good account of themselves. Rawdon declined, however, and Greene then fell back on the old Camden battlefield three miles to the north, leaving Rawdon in command of the battlefield. Rawdon did not pursue Greene, and indeed soon himself retired to the Camden defenses. In the battle, the casualties were about even. American losses totaled 270: 19 killed, 115 wounded, and 136 missing. British casualties came to 258: 38 killed and some 220 wounded or missing. Greene was not pleased with the outcome. He believed that the battle should have been his. He blamed Gunby alone and confessed that the battle's result had left him "almost frantick with vexation at the disappointment."

Greene's mood was reflected in a decision after the battle. His men caught several dozen American deserters. Greene had them court-martialed, and, when they were found guilty, ordered five of them hanged. Greene was both angry and depressed. Bitter as the pill of Rawdon's tactical victory might have been, Greene's army was still very much intact, and it was this battle that prompted Greene to remark in a letter to Washington, "We fight get beat and fight again." On May 3, Greene, short of food, withdrew to the southwest across the Wateree River. There he would be in position to threaten Rawdon's lines of communication.

CHAPTER ELEVEN

FORT MOTTE AND NINETY SIX

THE BATTLE OF HOBKIRK'S HILL, WHILE DISAPPOINTING TO Greene, did not change the strategic situation, nor did it much affect Greene's own plans. Following it, partisans under Sumter and Marion as well as Lee's Legion continued to operate against the British lines of communication and the Loyalists. Sumter, however, continued his unreliable ways, operating largely on his own and only occasionally obeying Greene's orders. Marion was quite the opposite and completely reliable. Meanwhile, despite the arrival of 500 reinforcements at Camden on May 7, Rawdon decided to abandon that post, departing on May 10. As a sign of the emptiness of the British victory of Hobkirk's Hill, during the ensuing five weeks, Patriot militiamen and Lee's Legion captured a number of British outposts.

The news of Rawdon's evacuation of Camden reenergized Greene. On May 11, Sumter took the important town of Orangeburg on the Edisto River, south of Camden. The next day, May 12, Marion and Lee laid siege to Fort Motte north of Orangeburg at the confluence of the Congaree and Wateree Rivers. Acting on Greene's orders, they hoped to secure it before Rawdon could come to the rescue. The garrison at Fort Motte numbered about 150 men, and the British had fortified the principal house on the Motte plantation, so it was impossible for Marion and Lee to take it without artillery. Mrs. Motte, owner of the plantation, had taken refuge in a nearby farmhouse. With Rawdon's force then just across the Congaree, Marion suggested to Mrs. Motte that the only way the Americans could take the British position was by setting the house on fire with flaming arrows to its roof. Reportedly, Mrs. Motte did not hesitate but handed him a bow and some arrows that were in the farmhouse. The story may not be true, but the Americans did set fire to the structure, forcing the British to evacuate it and taking them prisoner. Just at this moment, Greene and a half dozen aides rode up. It was Greene's first meeting with Marion.

On May 13, Greene sent Lee to the northwest against Fort Granby at the confluence of the Congaree and Saluda Rivers. Lee had only one small artillery piece with him, but three shots from it were sufficient to bring a British surrender that same day. Rawdon now decided to withdraw to Charleston so that he would not be cut off from his principal base. Greene, meanwhile, ordered Marion to strike the British post at Georgetown up the coast from Charleston. On the way to Georgetown, Marion harassed Rawdon's withdrawal as far as Monck's Corner, then hurried on to Georgetown, hoping to take it by surprise, but on May 29 its garrison withdrew to Charleston.

Greene could be pleased at what his men had accomplished. In the span of one month, the Americans had taken four British outposts and forced the evacuation of two others. By May 24 his men had taken 850 prisoners, including 50 officers, all of whom he sent under guard to North Carolina and western Virginia. Apart from Charleston, only one British post, Ninety Six, remained in South Carolina.

Greene's greatest need at this time was horses, both for his small cavalry units and to move riflemen quickly. He appealed to Jefferson in Virginia, but the legislature there had passed a law that made it difficult to impress horses for the Continental Army. In any case, Tarleton and Cornwallis seized all mounts they could find. Greene sought to prevail on Marion, but Marion replied that this was not in his power and chose to consider it an affront to his patriotism, threatening to go to Philadelphia and seek another assignment. Greene managed to mollify his subordinate, assuring Marion that he meant no slight and that he was providing invaluable service right where he was.

Greene also continued to experience problems with Sumter, who was not getting along with Lee. Sumter was especially upset that Lee had taken Fort Granby, which he had counted on securing himself. Indeed, Sumter might easily have accomplished that had he not been distracted by attacking and looting British supply columns. Greene was not fond of Sumter and his well-demonstrated disobedience, but the South Carolinian was too useful a guerrilla leader to lose. Sumter also threatened to resign, but Greene managed to mollify him as well. Perhaps more important in bringing Sumter around was the fact that Lee was no longer operating independently, but was serving as the vanguard of the army under Greene's personal command. Also Greene made Sumter titular head of militia in South Carolina. In truth, however, Sumter's usefulness was largely at an end.

Greene was determined to do all that he could to prevent atrocities being committed by the Patriot side against Tories. He was particularly upset by outrages committed against Tories of central South Carolina by men under Patriot militia Colonel LeRoy Hammond. Greene wrote to General Andrew Pickens, urging him to do all he could to halt attacks and reprisals that he believed to be seriously undermining the American cause. As he put to Pickens, "The Idea of exterminating the Tories is no less barbarous than impolitick; and if persisted in, will keep this Country in the greatest confusion and distress."

By mid-May, Greene was ready to move against the chief remaining British strongholds of Augusta and Ninety Six. On May 16, Greene ordered Lee to advance on Augusta. Lee arrived there on May 19 to find Pickens and Major Jonathan Clark of Virginia and their men already in place. Again the Americans constructed a large wooden tower, from which riflemen were able to fire into the fort. Augusta surrendered on June 5, the Americans taking prisoner its garrison of 350 British troops and Tory militiamen, as well as 300 Creek Indians.

On May 22, meanwhile, Greene had begun his own siege operations against Ninety Six, just west of the Saluda River. This operation ran the risk of attracting Rawdon, but Greene seemed to have welcomed the chance for a battle with him before taking Ninety Six. Rawdon did not oblige, however.

Ninety Six lay in lush, heavily Tory agricultural country coveted by both sides, but the fort was also of no use to Rawdon once the other British outposts had been lost. Indeed, Rawdon had sent orders to Ninety Six's commanding officer, Colonel John Harris Cruger, to withdraw to Augusta. Patriot guerrillas had, however, intercepted the couriers, with the result that the orders never reached Cruger.

Cruger commanded 50 British regulars and 350 Tory provincials and militia. The fort consisted of an old stockade, but Cruger had strengthened it by adding surrounding redoubts and abatis (sharpened stakes set in the ground that angled outward toward the attacker). The fort also boasted covered access to an ample water supply, essential in a siege.

By May 25, Greene's men had invested Ninety Six. Convinced that he could not take the fort by assault, Greene ordered Kosciuszko to begin siege operations. The siege was directed against an earthen outwork known as the Star Fort. The Polish engineer supervised the digging of parallels that edged ever closer to the British lines to enable the siting of cannon. Greene was not optimistic, writing Lafayette: "We have laid siege to this place but the fortifications are so strong and the garrison so large and so well furnished that our success is very doubtful."

Although Cruger attempted several sorties, the Americans beat them all back. Greene, meanwhile, ordered construction of a wooden tower similar to that employed successfully at Augusta. From it American riflemen fired into the fort. British attempts from the fort to set the tower alight with incendiaries failed against its green wood. On June 8, Lee came up with his dragoons, fresh from taking Augusta, and within four days had almost cut off the British water supply.

Eighteen days into the siege the Americans appeared on the brink of taking Ninety Six. That evening, June 12, however, a lone rider arrived. Spurring his horse, he rode through the American lines before he could be shot down and galloped into the British fort. The rider turned out to be a courier with news that Rawdon was on his way with a sizeable relief force. Greene had in fact himself learned of Rawdon's relief effort six days earlier and had sent out orders to both Marion and Sumter to delay the British. Only a few of Greene's immediate staff knew of the situation, which now was a race between the besiegers and the relief force.

The arrival of the courier was a fatal blow, encouraging Cruger to hold out as long as was absolutely possible. Also, Sumter had again disobeyed Greene's orders. He remained at Fort Granby on the Wateree River in the belief that Rawdon might move there. Rawdon was thus able to place his own men between those of Sumter and Greene. Greene had only 1,000 men to Rawdon's 2,000, which included the flank companies of three fresh British regiments. Receiving word that Rawdon was near, Greene yielded to pleas from his subordinates for one last effort to take Ninety Six. As Greene had feared, however, the American assault on June 18 failed with heavy loss in fierce hand-to-hand fighting outside the fortification.

Greene now had no choice but to withdraw. The first setback of the campaign, the siege of Ninety Six had lasted twenty-eight days and cost the Americans 185 men killed and wounded. Although some of his officers suggested that they again withdraw behind the Dan, Greene rejected this. Moving north well ahead of the pursuing Rawdon, Greene merely withdrew across the Broad River. Rawdon then evacuated Ninety Six and fell back toward Charleston. Greene followed before taking up position in the High Hills of Santee, a long chain of irregular hills northeast of Charleston on the east bank of the Wateree River south of Camden. The climate on the plateau was far healthier for the men, and the water there was pure. Here he hoped to rest and train his men and rebuild his forces.

Greene was furious at both Sumter, who he believed had cost him victory at Ninety Six, and also at Jefferson and the Virginia government, for failing to supply required horses and men. On arrival at his camp, Greene issued orders for a rigid regimen of training and exercise. On July 16, he insisted roll be called four times a day to guard against desertions, and he specified daily parade and regular guard duty. Good news came in the form of fresh horses, which had begun to arrive in camp.

Greene now moved against illegal requisitions in the lowlands, and he continued to express the view that Tories must be treated in such manner that after the war they would want to return to their homes and farms. He ordered Colonel Wade Hampton, a new partisan officer, to bring in captured plunderers to be tried by a military court.

It was an unpleasant business. South Carolina was in fact being ravaged by the war. Greene wrote to Caty: "Here turn which way you will, you have nothing but the mournful widow, and the plaints of the fatherless Child; and behold nothing but houses desolated, and plantations laid waste. Ruin is in every form, and misery in every shape."

CHAPTER TWELVE

EUTAW SPRINGS

ALTHOUGH HE HAD WON NO BATTLES DURING THE PERIOD of April to July 1781, Greene could reflect on solid accomplishments, for he now controlled the entire South Carolina interior. Although the backcountry remained largely lawless, the Tories were completely demoralized, with the British restricted to the two coastal enclaves of Charleston and Savannah. Rawdon pursued Greene for a while from Ninety Six but soon gave up the chase as a consequence of the heat and lack of provisions and returned to Ninety Six. Then on July 3, he ordered that place abandoned and its defenders and their families removed with his army, first to Orangeburg and then to Charleston. Dispirited and in poor health, there Rawdon handed over his command to Lieutenant Colonel Alexander Stewart, commander of the 3rd British Regiment, and sailed for England. Unfortunately for Rawdon, his ship was captured by the French, and, in consequence, he became a witness to the British defeat in the naval Battle of the Chesapeake that sealed the fate of Cornwallis, his former commander, at Yorktown.

Greene reflected on the recent events in a letter of July 18 to his friend Jeremiah Wadsworth. Noting that there were those who had criticized him for his retreating, Greene observed: "There are few Generals that has run oftner, or more lustily, than I have done, But I have taken care not to run too farr; and commonly have run as fast forward as backward, to convince our Enemy that we were like a Crab, that could run either way." Greene was no doubt pleased to receive praise from the commander in chief. Washington wrote him on June 1, "The difficulties which you daily encounter and surmount with your small force add not a little to your reputation." Meanwhile, on Greene's appeal, Governor John Rutledge returned to South Carolina. He established a civil government in Greene's camp in the High Hills of Santee, and his first act was a prohibition on plundering.

For several months, Greene worked at training and strengthening his forces. He maintained his strict discipline, including hanging soldiers for desertion and dismissing officers who failed to carry out their duties or obey orders. Sumter continued to be a problem. In one raid "the Gamecock" captured seven hundred gold guineas. Instead of turning the money over to Greene to be used for the benefit of the entire army, he divided it up among his own men and then disbanded his brigade. Greene sent Colonel Patterson to try to restore some military order in Sumter's wake and especially to prevent plundering.

Stewart, meanwhile, largely left the initiative to the Americans. He set up his own camp at the junction of the Wateree and Congaree Rivers, only about sixteen miles from Greene. The two armies were, however, separated by impassable swamps.

Never one to remain on the defensive for long, Greene was determined to attack Stewart, although to get to him the Americans would have to march some seventy miles. On August 22, his exertions having brought the strength of his army up to about 2,000 men, Greene marched north from the Santee Hills for Camden. He then crossed the Wateree before heading south for Eutaw Springs. The days were hot, and Greene's army moved only in the mornings and late afternoons. At Eutaw Springs, Stewart commanded some 2,000 men, but the great majority of them were regulars, including the 3rd, 63rd, and 64th Regiments, as well as Colonel John Cruger's garrison from Ninety Six. The British also had four artillery pieces.

On August 28, Greene reached Motte's plantation on the Congaree. Stewart, meanwhile, withdrew on Eutaw Springs on the Santee River. Greene enjoyed one great advantage over Stewart: superior information of enemy intentions. Sending back all of his supply wagons save two, Greene pressed forward.

Two days later, on August 30, Marion rejoined Greene, flush with success. That same day, in a highly successful hit-and-run raid, he had laid an ambush on the causeway leading to the ferry and defeated 300 British and Hessian infantry and 80 dragoons, as well as some Tories. At a cost to themselves of only 4 killed and wounded, the Americans had killed 20 and wounded 80, and also captured 40 horses. On September 7, Greene received welcome reinforcements in the form of South Carolina militiamen, bringing his total strength up to about 2,600 men, some half of who were Continentals. But of the total, only about 2,000 men were fit for frontline duty.

In a significant indication of the decline of British fortunes in the region, Loyalist support had all but vanished, enabling Greene to approach within easy range of the British camp before Stewart was aware of their presence. No friendly civilians rode to give the alarm. Indeed, on the night of September 7, the Americans camped only seven miles from Stewart.

On September 8, Greene had the army up at 4 a.m. and on the march. As they set out, a courier arrived with a message from Washington informing him that he and Rochambeau were on a forced march south to Yorktown. Admiral de Grasse was already in Chesapeake Bay with his fleet blocking Cornwallis from withdrawal by water. Greene did not have long to savor this good news. Another courier soon rode up, this one from Lee, informing Greene that they had encountered the British. Indeed, firing could be heard ahead.

Stewart had sent out a cavalry detachment of some 100 men under Major John Coffin to investigate a report from two American deserters that Greene was moving against Eutaw Springs. Stewart then became alarmed when a party of men he had sent out to dig sweet potatoes failed to return. Sighting Lee's Legion, Coffin's men had ridden up to investigate, instigating the fighting.

Lee deployed his region across the road and sent his militiamen into a thicket on one side. Greene soon heard the advance guard galloping back on the rest of the American army. Thinking he was chasing down militia, Coffin had pursued, only to have the Americans halt and turn about, laying down a deadly fire. As the British tried to flee, they found their way blocked by Lee's cavalrymen, who had gotten behind them, and by Lee's infantrymen with the bayonet. The British then fled into the woods. During the melee, Greene rode forward to assess the situation and soon found himself in the middle of the fight. The noise of the skirmish drew the foraging party back to the road. Informed by an aide that there were British to his rear, Greene instructed him to tell the British that unless they surrendered, he would have his cavalry ride them down. The British complied. In the skirmish, the Americans captured 40 of Coffin's men.

Stewart now quickly deployed his force at Eutaw Springs. He had chosen an excellent defensive position, for the British camp was bounded on the right by the high banks of Eutaw Creek, which was also bordered by thick brush and undergrowth. The only open ground was on both sides of the road. A rearward approach was impossible because beyond the cleared fields there was a mass of deep hollows and thick blackjack shrub. A well-constructed two-story brick house with garret windows, in effect a third story, dominated the cleared area, and the farm's barn and other outbuildings offered other potential defensive firing points. The British camp was on either side of the road. Stewart deployed his men in single line about one hundred yards in advance of the encampment, confident that they would be able to defeat the advancing Americans. A flank battalion of light infantry and grenadiers guarded the right flank near Eutaw Creek, while Coffin commanded a mixed force of cavalry and infantry on the British left, both as a flank guard and Stewart's only reserve.

Greene also deployed in line. As in prior engagements, he arranged his men in two ranks, the militia in front, hoping that they could weaken the defenders and that he would then be able to use his Continentals at the decisive spot. In the center of the militia line, he placed the most reliable of these units, a North Carolina contingent under the French volunteer officer the Marquis de Malmédy. Marion's South Carolina partisans held Greene's right, while Pickens's South Carolina partisans were on the left. In the second rank of Continentals, Lieutenant Colonel Richard

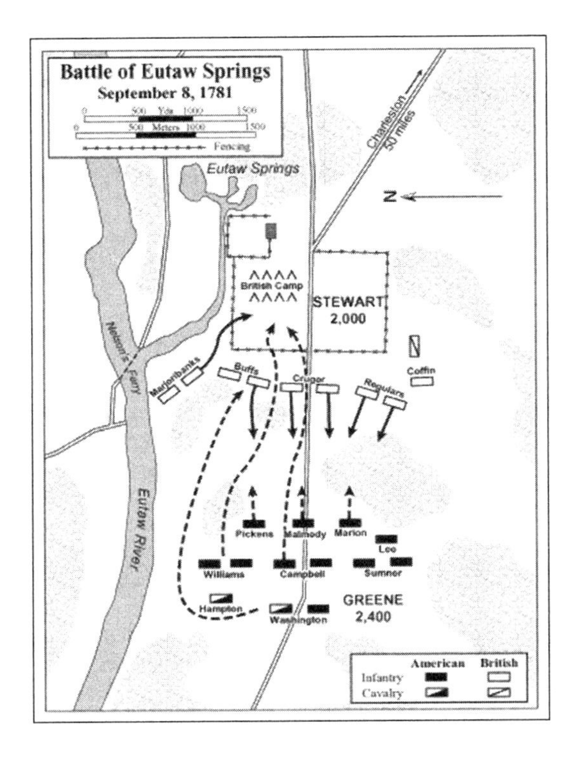

Campbell's Virginians were in the center; the right was held by a new North Carolina brigade under Major General Jethro Sumner, and Colonel Otho Williams's Maryland brigade held the left flank. Lee's Legion of cavalry and infantry protected Greene's right flank, while Lieutenant Colonel William Henderson's South Carolina infantry and Colonel Wade Hampton's cavalry protected the Continental left. Greene held in reserve William Washington's dragoons and Captain Robert Kirkwood's Delaware Continental infantry. Greene had four guns: two 3-pounders and two 6-pounders.

Greene advanced his two lighter artillery pieces forward. Quickly unlimbered, these tore large holes in the British line until both were disabled. One of the British 3-pounders was also put out of action. Lee's Legion and Henderson's men were both heavily engaged and held their respective flanks. Henderson was later wounded and had to leave the field, his place taken by Hampton.

This time the Patriot militia, led by Pickens and Marion, fought well. Only Malmédy's North Carolina militia broke and ran. Greene then sent Sumner's untested North Carolina Continentals to fill this gap in the first line. They reestablished the line and engaged the British until they too were driven back in a British bayonet charge. Greene still had available his best troops, the Maryland and Virginia regiments that had fought at Guilford Court House and Hobkirk's Hill. Ordered forward at the double, they met the onrushing British, blunted their attack, and then steadily forced the British back. Meanwhile, Lee had opened an enfilading fire on the British, his infantry turning the British left flank. The battle was hard fought, and in his report to Congress, Greene was full of praise for his men. He said he "could hardly tell which to admire most the gallantry of their Officers or the bravery of the Troops. They kept up a heavy and well directed fire, and the Enemy returned it with equal spirit, for they really fought worthy of a better cause, and great execution was done on both sides."

This was the decisive point in the battle. The Maryland and Virginia Continentals now pushed forward. The British, exhausted, were soon in full retreat, withdrawing to their camp and moving even beyond. Some retreated down the Charleston Road. Greene seemed to be on the verge of decisive victory. It was not to be, for when the Americans entered the British camp, many of the men stopped to plunder the British supplies. This broke up the attack. Lee's Legion continued, taking prisoners, but it operated virtually alone.

British Major John Marjoribanks seized the opportunity. Greene had ordered Washington's cavalry to circle around the American left against Marjoribanks. But Washington's men charged without waiting for Kirkwood's infantry support. On the far left and isolated from the remainder of the Continentals, they found themselves cut off. Unable to penetrate the thicket, Washington and some of his officers had their horses shot from under them by Marjoribanks's men, and Washington, who was wounded, was taken prisoner as he struggled to free himself from his stirrups.

Kirkwood's Delaware troops and Hampton's mounted men arrived just as Major Henry Sheridan and the New York Volunteers took up position in the brick house east of the British camp. There they opened up a deadly fire on the American infantry emerging from the camp. Stewart rallied his men on the south of the camp while Greene even brought up his artillery, but the small American field pieces proved useless against the well-built brick residence. Stewart now rallied his men as the Americans tried to take the brick house. Once his troops were reformed, Stewart counter-attacked. Seeing the infantry advancing, Coffin joined the attack on the British left. As the British swept through the camp, Marjoribanks joined the attack on the right. Hampton then arrived and halted the British in a saber-on-saber fight, driving them back to the vicinity of the brick house, but when Hampton himself retired to reorganize, Coffin reemerged and made for the American artillery pieces. Cutting down the artillerymen with their sabers, the British seized the American guns and rode off with them.

By this time, Stewart had reestablished his line. As soon as Greene had learned that his men had broken ranks in the British camp, he had unbent every effort to restore order. At length, Greene was able to reform the men, but his own force was now utterly exhausted after four hours of battle and was so thoroughly disorganized that he knew he had no option but to withdraw. His men then marched the seven miles back to their camp.

Although the Battle of Eutaw Springs ended in another draw, Greene had come very close to a decisive victory. Losses were heavy on both sides in what was indeed the hardest fought of all battles in the American South during the war. With 522 casualties, the Americans lost some 25 percent of their force: 139 killed, including 17 officers; 375 wounded; and 8 missing. Of Greene's 6 top commanders, only Lee and Otho Williams came through the battle unscathed. But Stewart's losses were much heavier, amounting to more than 40 percent of his force. The British sustained 866 casualties: 85 killed, 351 wounded, and 430 missing, including prisoners. Indeed, Stewart was so weakened by the battle that he had no option but to withdraw back to Monck's Corner just north of Charleston. He left the day after the battle, abandoning 70 of his most severely wounded under a flag of truce to be cared for by the Americans. Greene at first pursued but, learning that Stewart had been reinforced, broke off the effort.

No doubt embarrassed at yet again leaving the enemy in possession of the field, Greene reported that he had left behind "on the field of action" a "strong Piquett" force to keep watch on the British. This was certainly not true. More probable was the claim to have recovered 1,000 "stands of Arms." Also not true was Greene's claim to Lafayette that he had "obtained a complete victory." This misses the point, which is contained in the earlier characterization of North Carolina Governor Abner Nash to Greene that he possessed "the peculiar Art of making your Enemies run away from their Victories leaving you master of their Wounded and of all the fertile part of the Country."

Washington was fulsome in praise of Greene, and so were congressional leaders, many of whom had earlier been critical of Greene and even sought his dismissal. All believed Eutaw Springs to have been a great victory. Indeed, Congress now voted Greene a gold medal for his accomplishments.

The Battle of Eutaw Springs was the last major engagement in the war in the South. Patriot civilian administration was slowly but steadily being restored in the deep South, and although fighting still raged in the interior between irregular forces, the British were restricted to a handful of coastal enclaves. For all practical purposes, Eutaw Springs marks the end of Greene's long effort to regain the southern states.

Greene detached Lee and Marion to watch Stewart, and, his own strength down to only 1,000 effectives, again withdrew to the Santee Hills. On September 17, Greene wrote to Washington that he believed Charleston might be taken in the fashion of Yorktown, "if you bend your forces this way; and it will afford me great pleasure to Join your Excellency in the Attempt for I shall be equally happy, whether as principal or subordinate so that the Public good is promoted."

CHAPTER THIRTEEN

END OF THE WAR

TO THE NORTH IN VIRGINIA, THE DECISIVE BATTLE OF THE war was occurring at Yorktown on Chesapeake Bay. Greene, always thinking in strategic terms, had written to Washington on June 22, 1781, when he learned that Cornwallis had committed himself to Virginia, that this would be an excellent opportunity to bag Cornwallis. He thought it could be accomplished in three weeks, whereas taking either New York or Charleston would be "long[,] tedious and uncertain."

When Admiral de Grasse sailed to the Chesapeake, Washington marched the bulk of his own army and the allied French forces south, and Cornwallis found himself blockaded by sea and land. The allied siege began on September 28, and Cornwallis formally surrendered some 7,000 British soldiers on October 19, 1781 (the three weeks that Greene had predicted). The event was tumultuous, ending the British plan to prosecute the war until victory was achieved. Hard-line prime minister Lord North resigned, and the ministry that succeeded him headed by Charles Watson-Wentworth, second Marquis of Rockingham, embarked on a new policy of cutting British losses. The new ministry took the position that France was the real enemy and that Britain should befriend the United States, even to the extent of giving it additional territory, in order to prevent it from falling into the French orbit.

Greene's private reaction to his chief's glorious victory is an interesting one, for it again reveals the depth of his own great thirst for military glory. In a letter to his close friend Henry Knox, he praised Washington's success but noted:

> We have been beating the bush and the General has come to catch the bird. Never was there a more inviting object to glory. The General is a most fortunate Man, and may success and laurels attend him. We have fought frequently and bled freely, and little glory comes to our share. Our force has been so small that nothing capital could be effected, and our operations have been conducted under every disadvantage that could embarrass either a General or an Army.

Meanwhile, Greene repeatedly appealed to Congress and the state governments for assistance. He wrote to the Board of War in late November 1781, "We are also in the greatest distress for want of almost everything in the quarter Masters department. . . . We are oblige to broil most of our meat for want of Camp Kettles to cook in. We are in the greatest distress for want of shoes. We cannot march without Shoes nor can we fight without Ammunition."

Greene's requests for aid, even vital hospital supplies, went unanswered. Increasingly he was forced to rely on a barter system. Thus he allowed militiamen to depart before their terms had expired on the promise that they would fashion a set number of canteens and horseshoes for army use. He also exchanged goods such as indigo and tobacco for clothing.

At the same time Greene rejected a chance to leave his field command for Philadelphia. Gouverneur Morris wrote Greene that he was being considered for the new post of secretary of war. Congress was now ready to embrace a man it had sought to fire earlier. But mutually shared combat and privation had forged a bond between Greene and his men that would be hard to break, short of final victory. Besides, his earlier visits to Philadelphia had not been happy, and indeed had left him angry, frustrated, and discouraged. Greene responded to Morris on November 21: "You think I am fond of an Army and a busy scene. You mistake my feelings. I am truly domestic. The more I am in the Army and the more I am acquainted with human Nature the less fond I am of political life." Besides, Greene said he was "poor," and he was determined, once the war was over, to do everything he could to build up his personal fortune. He could hardly support his growing family on a government salary. Whatever Greene's chances might have been, Congress eventually appointed Benjamin Lincoln to the post.

Despite Greene's efforts to end it, fighting between Tory and Patriot still raged in the South. In a brazen effort to disrupt civilian government and reinvigorate their flagging cause, Tories captured Patriot governor and friend of Greene, Thomas Burke, as well as some other North Carolina officials, turning them over to the British. Alexander Martin soon replaced Burke as acting governor, however, and the situation quickly stabilized, but this did not end the cruel Tory-on-Patriot atrocities, and no matter how much he said he disliked politics, Greene found himself drawn into them as he endeavored to end the civil war.

For the most part, Greene urged a policy of reconciliation rather than retribution. When he learned of outrages committed by Patriots against Tories by troops under North Carolina militia brigadier general Griffith Rutherford, he wrote Rutherford spelling out his position in no uncertain terms. Greene acknowledged that while Patriots had good reason to feel resentment against the Tories, revenge was not the answer: "In national concerns as well as in private life passion is a bad councellor and resentment an unsafe guide." If influenced by these, they produce acts of "the most horid cruelty. . . . If we persue the Tories indiscriminately and drive them to a state [of] desperation we shall make them from a weak and feeble force a sure and determined enemy." Greene regarded cruelty not only as dishonorable, but certain to increase the ranks of those opposing independence.

Greene urged conciliatory measures, including pardons for some Tories. Although South Carolina governor John Rutledge did so, North Carolina acting governor Alexander Martin refused. Greene did not press the matter, noting, "We Military Men can only advise and not dictate in these matters."

Many in the country assumed the war was all but over after the Battle of Yorktown; Washington and Greene were not among them. On November 8, 1781, three weeks after the British surrender at Yorktown, with his army still short of vital supplies, and aware that he would receive no major land reinforcements, Greene resumed offensive operations. He did not plan to fight another set-piece battle similar to Eutaw Springs, but a series of small engagements in which he might whittle away British strength. Toward this end he left Otho Williams in command of his camp and took 400 men—half Lee's and Washington's cavalrymen and half Maryland and Virginia Continental infantry—and personally led them against some 850 British troops at Dorchester, South Carolina, the last British outpost north of Charleston. Major General Alexander Leslie had now succeeded Stewart in command of British forces in the South at Charleston.

Some skirmishing occurred en route, with the Americans arriving at Dorchester on December 1. Greene was recognized leading the force, and the British commander there incorrectly assumed that meant that the entire Southern Army was present and that he was outnumbered. He ordered stores burnt, his guns thrown into Ashley River, and the troops to withdraw to Charleston.

The British were now confined to Charleston and Savannah, and Greene's campaign was essentially over. The British were reluctant to go after Greene, while Greene lacked the strength to take the major British positions. In early December, however, Greene repositioned his army between the two British southern coastal enclaves at a location known as "Round O" some thirty-five miles west of Charleston.

In these circumstances, rumors began to circulate and reached the American camp to the effect that a large number of British reinforcements were on their way from New York and Ireland to Charleston, and that these would enable the British soon to take the offensive. Greene's response was a radical one. African-American troops having proven themselves on the Patriot side in fighting in the North, Greene proposed to take advantage of their large numbers in the South to raise four regiments there, and to give freedom to the slaves who enlisted. He wrote to Governor Rutledge noting that no help was to be expected from the North in time and that this seemed the only real way to raise a large number of men quickly because of the poor state of South Carolina's finances and the small number of whites living in the state. Greene went on to praise the fighting qualities of African-Americans: "That they would make good Soldiers I have not the least doubt. . . . Should this measure be adopted, It may prove a great means of preventing the Enemy from further attempts upon this country, when they find they have not only the whites, but the blacks also to contend with."

Needless to say, Greene's proposal was a non-starter, meeting adamant resistance from white leaders. There were those in the state who saw in the proposal a hidden agenda by a Northern abolitionist. As events would regrettably prove, however, Greene was not one. South Carolina leaders also opposed Greene's suggestions that post-conflict healing would be facilitated if lands were returned to those Tories who agreed to provide information on the British. It was during the consideration of a slave-enlistment bill that Greene's friend Governor Rutledge secured passage of a bill that awarded Greene a plantation, one of many confiscated from Tories, for his great services to the state. Greene accepted this property, worked by slaves, apparently with no reservations.

The victory at Yorktown at last enabled Washington to reinforce Greene, and in January 1782, 2,000 Maryland and Pennsylvania troops under Major General Arthur St. Clair arrived at Round O. On January 9, Greene dispatched Brigadier General Anthony Wayne, who had been fighting with Lafayette in Virginia, south with two regiments of Pennsylvania Continentals and an artillery detachment in order to free Georgia from British control. Wayne performed very well, although only narrowly escaping annihilation in an Indian attack.

Greene was also heartened by the arrival in late March 1782 of Caty at his camp at Round O plantation, ending their longest separation of the war. Caty Greene was escorted south by a group of officers personally selected by General Washington. At Round

O, Caty rode often with Greene, and she endeared herself to the men by her frequent presence in military hospitals looking after the sick. Certainly she did much to lift Greene's spirits.

General Sir Guy Carleton succeeded Clinton as commander of British troops in America on May 9, 1782. Then, in June 1782, Leslie sent out feelers for an armistice. Greene summarily rejected this, claiming that power rested only with Congress. He himself believed an armistice could come only with the consent of France. Carleton, meanwhile, concentrated his forces in New York, evacuating Wilmington in January, Savannah in July, and Charleston in December.

Greene maintained his army in the vicinity of Charleston but did not attempt to attack the British there. Neither did Washington move against New York in the north. Apart from small raids, both sides adopted a policy of waiting for the politicians to sort out the peace settlement. Greene's attention shifted to matters of supply. His army was short of all major supplies, even clothing. In August 1782, Greene informed Superintendent of Finance Robert Morris that for two months a third of his men had been "entirely naked," wearing breechcloths only, and were thus reluctant to leave their tents, while the remainder were "as ragged as wolves." Food was also in short supply, for the locals were now insisting on payment in hard money and gold. Meat was hard to come by, and such beef as was available was "perfect carrion."

The summer of 1782 was especially difficult, for widespread malaria claimed the lives of hundreds of Greene's men. On August 26, Greene issued an order that forbade the beating of the dead march for funerals, as it was depressing the spirits of the men. As a sign that the war was almost over, Greene was able to work out an arrangement with General Leslie that allowed some of the sick Americans to recover on British-controlled Kiawah Island off Charleston. Caty Greene joined them for a time, helping to restore their spirits.

Greene's last months as commander in the South, from December 1782 through August 1783, were difficult. Most of his soldiers were from the mid-Atlantic states, and they were anxious to return to their homes before the arrival of another malaria season. The men became increasingly restive, especially with a peace settlement near. Troops from Pennsylvania nearly mutinied in late April. Although Greene admitted that the men's complaints were justified, he would tolerate no insubordination in the ranks, and he ordered the mutineer ringleader tried and hanged. This had the desired effect of cowing the remainder of the malcontents.

At the same time, the war-weary southern states believed peace to be imminent and were therefore reluctant to make the financial decisions required to feed and supply Greene's army. Yet these same governments were unwilling to see the army depart before peace was actually concluded. In the North, units of the Continental Army were fed and clothed on a contractual arrangement, while in the South, Greene was obliged to rely entirely on the states, which for the most part simply failed to carry out their obligations. The burden of sustaining the army fell to the South Carolina government, and even Wayne in Georgia was forced to rely on it for supplies. Yet those citizens who had goods to sell inevitably traded with the British who paid for them in specie.

John Banks, representing the mercantile firm of Banks and Hunter of Fredericksburg, Virginia, offered to provide goods for the Southern Army at a high price, in return for which he demanded a safe conduct pass that would get him through the British lines to trade in Charleston. Greene refused to treat with him. But with conditions worsening in the American camp, rumors of mutiny surfaced, and a woman informant told Greene of a plot to kidnap him and other leading officers and turn them over to the British. Allegedly the plot included a British cavalry unit that would be positioned near the American camp to spirit away the prisoners. The informant named the ringleaders, and Greene immediately had them arrested. Placed on trial, they were found guilty, sentenced to be executed, and hanged before the entire army. This action, however, did nothing to alleviate the dire camp conditions. Dysentery broke out in the camp, and foraging, even if done by force, was insufficient to supply the army's needs. Greene had the authority to secure clothing and provisions, but he had no means to pay for them. Although peace negotiations were underway, these were not a sure thing, and the British still held Charleston and could resume the war at any time. The Southern Army had to be held together until peace had been secured.

In these dire circumstances, Greene reluctantly agreed to treat with Banks. He and George Abbott Hall, a secret agent of Robert Morris, met with the merchant. After considerable haggling, Hall agreed to advance Banks seven hundred guineas from gold available for emergency use only. This was to be partly payment for clothing Banks secured on the black market in Charleston. While the army was now better clothed, it still suffered from near starvation. Banks agreed to provide food, and again there was great discussion, in which he agreed to reduce his price. But with Banks pressed by creditors, the suppliers agreed to produce the food only if Greene would personally guarantee payment.

Even the staunch patriot Greene must have hesitated, for he would be putting his own financial future in jeopardy. The state of South Carolina had rewarded his services with the gift of the large plantation of Boone's Barony on the Edisto River. The plantation itself had once belonged to royal governor Thomas Boone. The legislature authorized ten thousand guineas to buy the land, but it cost less than that, and Greene successfully petitioned to use the rest of the money to buy the plantation's slaves. Georgia had also voted him the 2,100-acre Mulberry Grove plantation on the Savannah River, some fourteen miles from Savannah. It had been seized from the former Loyalist lieutenant governor, John Graham. North Carolina had also awarded him 2,500 acres. Greene readily accepted all these gifts. The grants no doubt helped to cement his decision to remain in the South after the war, where, after all, he was lionized as liberator.

Greene had earlier sold his holdings in Coventry to his brothers. His investments had turned out badly, and the sums and properties voted him by the southern states were now in fact his major financial assets. He would be risking everything if Banks failed to pay. In making the decision to pledge his own assets, Greene relied on the advice of two aides, Majors Robert Burnet and Robert Forsythe. Unknown to Greene, both men had secretly agreed to become silent business partners with Banks. They now urged Greene to sign, and, with the army starving, Greene agreed.

The arrangement between Banks and Greene's aides soon leaked out, and Greene's enemies sought to use this to prove that the general himself was involved. The evidence suggests he was not, for immediately on learning of this, Greene summoned Banks, and in the presence of both Wayne and Carrington, his chief of commissary, he had Banks swear under oath that Greene knew nothing of his arrangement with Burnet and Forsythe.

Finally, on December 14, 1782, the last of General Leslie's British troops departed Charleston, evacuated in three hundred ships to New York. Wayne, commanding 300 infantrymen, 80 cavalrymen, and two 6-pounder guns, was right behind. With the British safely aboard ship by 11 a.m., that afternoon Greene and Governor Mathews entered the city on horseback and rode between lines of Continental Army troops to the statehouse. In the evening there was a great ball to celebrate the return of Charleston, and Nathanael and Caty Greene were the center of attention.

According to the 1778 alliance with France, neither side was to conclude a separate peace; but the Americans did just that. By the Peace of 1783, although the British were still in possession of New York, and governments friendly to the new nation would just as soon have confined it east of the mountains, the new republic secured territory as far west as the Mississippi. In another major concession, the Americans were also to have full rights to the Newfoundland fisheries. Canada, however, remained British and received an English-speaking population by the settlement there of more than sixty thousand refugee Americans who had remained loyal to Great Britain, in many cases leaving all they owned behind them.

Not until April 30, 1783, did Greene learn of the preliminary convention of peace signed in Paris the previous November 30. Greene managed to hold together most of the army until transports could arrive to take them home, the last departing Charleston on July 29. Caty, pregnant again, traveled north by ship. Greene remained for a time alone. He noted in a letter, "I am left like Samson after Delilah cut his locks."

At last setting out on August 11, Greene, accompanied by several of his aides, traveled to Rhode Island overland, receiving accolades in Wilmington, Richmond, Baltimore, and Philadelphia. Reunited with Washington in Trenton, Greene traveled with him to Princeton, where Congress was then meeting after having fled Philadelphia and hundreds of disgruntled Pennsylvania soldiers demanding back pay. Congress voiced its thanks to Greene and accepted his resignation from the army.

His military career now over, Greene went on to Newport as a civilian, there to be reunited on November 17 with Caty and their four children. On Greene's arrival, the citizens of East Greenwich turned out in his honor with a parade by the Kentish Guards. The Rhode Island General Assembly traveled to East Greenwich for the occasion and met in the courthouse there to pay homage to the state's most distinguished citizen.

One of Greene's first priorities was to acquaint himself with the children he hardly knew. Years later, his daughter Cornelia described the ease with which Greene made the transition from staunch disciplinarian to loving, doting parent. "He was our boon companion and playfellow," Cornelia wrote, "who winked at every atrocity we precipitated."

Despite the joys of the reunion with his family, Greene was troubled about his personal financial situation. The Rhode Island businesses that were once his no longer belonged to him, and his investment of £10,000 with Deane in 1779 had depreciated to only £960. His sole wealth resided in the properties and money given him by South Carolina and Georgia.

CHAPTER FOURTEEN

LAST YEARS

WITH THE RETURN OF PEACE, GREENE, EVER THE NATIONAList, strongly urged the states to impose a 5 percent tax on trade in order to raise money to pay the great debt incurred during the war, Congress having no power to tax. Greene was chagrined, before he left the South, to see the state governments there refuse this, and even Rhode Island later followed suit. Greene also aligned himself firmly with Washington, Hamilton, Steuben, and others who testified before Congress in 1783 in favor of a small professional army for the new republic. This stance brought him into conflict with some of the more prominent localist political leaders in the South who had risen to power in the waning days of the war.

In the summer of 1784, Greene returned to South Carolina. He planned first to place Boone's Barony and then Mulberry Grove in good order and assure his financial future. It was thus a great blow for Greene to learn in the fall of 1784 that John Banks had gone bankrupt for $150,000 and that he was now responsible for the other man's debts. Banks fled to the interior. Greene set off after him to confront him, reportedly with two loaded pistols. No doubt, Greene hoped that Banks was concealing assets that could be used to make good on the debts. When Greene finally caught up with Banks, however, he found him dead and buried.

Greene then returned to Boone's Barony. He told Caty, "I tremble at my own situation when I think of the enormous sums I owe. I seem to be doomed to a life of slavery." There was no other recourse for Greene but to give up some of his holdings, and he sold the South Carolina plantation to satisfy the creditors.

It is indeed ironic that Greene's property could be made profitable only if worked by slave labor, for slavery was an institution that Greene, the former Quaker, said he abhorred. Nonetheless, he apparently had no misgivings about being a slave owner himself. He did voice on occasion his desire to try to keep slave families together. In January 1784, Greene wrote Robert Morris, "I find I can get my Georgia plantation stocked with good Gangs of Negroes at about $70 a head and the payments made mostly by installments if not all and those for a considerable length of time." He borrowed funds from both Morris and former commissary general Jeremiah Wadsworth to purchase slaves and equipment for Mulberry Grove.

Appointed by Congress in March 1784 to a commission to negotiate treaties with the Indians, Greene turned it down, for Caty was then experiencing a slow recovery from the birth of their fifth child, Louisa. Late that same month, however, Greene did not hesitate when he was invited to Philadelphia for the first meeting of the Society of the Cincinnati, composed of former officers of the Continental Army under the presidency of his mentor and hero George Washington.

Personal finances remained his chief concern. Greene planned to settle permanently at Mulberry Grove, but to spend the summers with his family in the North in a house he had purchased in Newport. In summer 1785, Caty gave birth to their sixth child, conceived when Greene was in Rhode Island in late 1784. The child was named Catharine after her mother. She developed a terrible cough and died that same summer.

In October 1785, Greene, Caty, and their surviving five children settled down at Mulberry Grove. It and its surrounding 2,141 acres had fallen into disrepair during the ten years since its previous owner had fled the country. A few years earlier, Greene had purchased a half-interest in Cumberland and Little Cumberland Islands off the southern coast of Georgia. There he hoped to cultivate the oak trees on the property for shipbuilders.

At the same time it had awarded Mulberry Grove to Greene, the state of Georgia had presented the neighboring Richmond and Kew plantation to Greene's subordinate and friend Anthony Wayne (appointed major general in October 1783), who had played an important role in defeating British forces in Georgia. Life seemed good. Greene turned down not only the opportunity to become secretary of war, but refused the offer of a Georgia judgeship and offers of posts in Rhode Island. After eight long years of war, he was tired of public service and anxious to secure his financial future.

Greene spent much time writing letters and spending his own funds to come to the aid of officers he believed had been wronged. He actively corresponded with Washington, Hamilton, and Robert Morris. And Greene strongly supported the effort to replace the confederation of states with a stronger federal, centralized government. To Robert Morris, he urged: "Call a convention of the States and establish a Congress upon a constitutional footing. Give them full powers to govern the empire, and make them accountable for their conduct."

Greene threw himself into the management of Mulberry Grove, which was large and had for the most part escaped wartime damage. Soon it was more productive than ever before. Outwardly, Greene appeared content. He wrote a friend in the North that "The prospect is delightful and the house magnificent." The plantation had a fine smokehouse, a coach house, good riding horses, an outkitchen, and a pigeon house that could accommodate one thousand birds. He and Caty enjoyed riding over the plantation's lands. The next spring, Greene wrote that they had sixty acres in corn, large strawberries, and an orchard with apples, pears, peaches, plums, nectarines, apricots, figs, and oranges.

Yet financial problems persisted. In August 1785 he wrote to Richard Henry Lee, asking him to petition Congress to assume the debts that Greene had incurred in the maintenance of the Southern Army. He admitted to longtime friend Henry Knox, "My family is in distress and I am overwhelmed with difficulties and God knows when or where they will end. I work hard and live poor but I fear all this will not extricate me." Knox and Alexander Hamilton endeavored to lobby on his behalf, but it was only seven years later, after Greene's death, that Congress took action.

Setbacks continued. Greene lost fifty barrels of rice to a fire and another fifty-five sank in the Savannah River. Then, in April 1786, Caty, again pregnant, fell and went into premature labor. The baby, born prematurely, died soon after its birth.

On June 12, 1786, Greene rode to Savannah with Caty to make a final payment to one of Bank's creditors. They spent that night in the home of one of his former aides, Captain Nathaniel Pendleton from Virginia, who had made his home in Savannah after the war. They left the city early the next morning, traveling in the cool of the day and expecting to reach Mulberry Grove before the day became oppressively hot. But Greene's newfound enthusiasm for his plantation led him to stop at a neighboring plantation on the way home, there to inspect its rice fields. He spent several hours examining the fields, but, unlike his host, failed to carry an umbrella to protect himself from the sun. That afternoon his head began to ache, and the next day he was in great pain from severe sunstroke. His doctors bled him, to no avail. All efforts to cure him failed, and he died on the morning of June 19, a month shy of his forty-fourth birthday.

Wayne had stayed with Greene most of the time since he had fallen ill. It was he who broke the news to the public. Following an Episcopal service, Greene was buried in a vault in Savannah cemetery. In 1902, however, his remains were removed and buried beneath the Greene monument in Johnson Square in Savannah.

On April 27, 1792, President Washington approved and signed an act that indemnified the Greene estate for the funds that Nathanael Greene had spent to clear the debt owed to merchants for maintenance of the Southern Army. That same year, Caty met young Eli Whitney. Invited to Mulberry Grove to pursue his inventions and serve as tutor, within a year he had produced a model for the cotton gin. In 1796, Caty married Phineas Miller, who had originally come to Georgia as Greene's secretary. Despite previous success and their best efforts, Mulberry Grove fell upon hard times by 1798, thanks in large part to money expended on financing Whitney's cotton gin firm and losses sustained by Miller in a land investment that went bad. Two years later, the Millers were forced to sell the plantation because of debt. They moved to Cumberland Island, where, in 1803, they built the four-story mansion Dungeness, which Greene himself had planned. Phineas Miller died the next year, and Caty remained at Dungeness, dying there on September 2, 1814.

AFTERWORD

NATHANAEL GREENE WAS ONE OF THE MOST IMPORTANT figures of the Revolutionary War, second only to George Washington in his generalship and accomplishments. Had he not died in 1786, he might have played a prominent role in the new republic. No doubt he would have joined Hamilton and Washington as an articulate spokesman for a strong central federal government. It also seems likely that Washington would have again sought his services, and most probably would have selected Greene over Wayne to train and command the new Legion of the United States, which became the United States Army. No doubt, as a result, his name would today be better known.

Greene's place in American military history is secure. Driven by an abiding patriotism, but also by a great thirst for military glory, he liberated the South and proved himself one of the great generals of American military history. Greene began the campaign in the midst of raging civil war, with few resources and no personal knowledge of the terrain. A gifted organizer, he took the cards dealt him and played them to maximum advantage. Relentless in his pursuit of victory and having nearly unbounded energy, he proved decisive in action.

Greene led by example. Seemingly indifferent to fatigue, he shared the discomforts of his men and did his best to insure their welfare. This included pledging his own fortune toward that end. He understood clearly the wants and needs of the common soldiers, and he knew that they could not be expected to fight unless they were taken care of.

Greene was a brilliant strategist, and his operations in the Carolinas remain one of the most masterly campaigns in U.S. military history and a useful study today. Greene effectively used the assets available to him. Reluctant to hazard his meager resources, he was a master logistician who planned his battles and campaigns carefully. He had an uncommon interest in geography and used this to his great advantage. Perhaps more than any other general of the Revolutionary War, Greene understood the value of partisan warfare and was able to integrate this effectively into his overall strategy. He also had an exquisite sense of timing, including when to give battle. In an engagement, he had the great abilities of being able to see the situation clearly and act accordingly. Personally brave, Greene did not hesitate to expose himself to danger in the fulfillment of his duties and encouragement of his men. Greene was also a strong disciplinarian, but in keeping with the norms of his day. He could neither abide disobedience nor stupidity. Certainly Greene sought personal fame. Loyalty mattered much to him, and he gave that completely to Washington. He idolized the American commander in chief, who was very much a father figure for him.

"Light Horse" Harry Lee summed up Greene when he wrote, "pure and tranquil from the consciousness of just intentions, the undisturbed energy of his mind was wholly devoted to the effectual accomplishment of the high trust reposed in him." Quite simply, Greene was the greatest of Washington's generals.

NOTES

Chapter One: Early Life to 1775

1. George Washington Greene, *The Life of Nathanael Greene, Major-General in the Army of the Revolution.* vol. 1. (New York: G. P. Putnam's Sons, 1867). vols. 2 and 3 (New York: Hard and Houghton, Riverside Press, 1871).
2. *The Papers of General Nathanael Greene* (Chapel Hill: The University of North Carolina Press, for the Rhode Island Historical Society, 1976), 1:48. [Hereafter cited as *PNG*]
3. Ibid., 1:49.
4. Ibid., 1:47.
5. G. W. Greene, *Life*, 28.
6. *PNG*, 1:9–10.
7. Greene's grandson discusses at length the books he read. See G. W. Greene, *Life*, 22–39.

Chapter Two: The Approach of War

1 . G. W. Greene, *Life*, 26–27.

2. Florence Parker Simister, *The Fire's Center: Rhode Island in the Revolutionary Era, 1763–1790* (Providence, RI: Rhode Island Bicentennial Foundation, 1979), 43–44.

3. On the *Gaspee* Affair, see John Russell Bartlett, *A History of the Destruction of His Britannic Majesty's Schooner Gaspee, in Narragansett Bay, on the 10th June, 1772* (Providence, RI: A. Crawford Greene, 1861).

4. *PNG*, 1:37–38.

5. *PNG*, 1:53.

6. *PNG*, 1:65.

7. *PNG*, 1:67–68.

8. *PNG*, 1:75–76.

9. Rhode Island Historical Society, Friends' Minutes, 1751–1806, in *PNG*, 1:69.

10. *PNG*, 1:75–76.

11. *PNG*, 1:78–79.

Chapter Three: Beginning of the War and the Siege of Boston

1. Robert Harvey, *A Few Bloody Noses: The Realities and Mythologies of the American Revolution* (NY: Overlook Press, 2002), 160.

2. *PNG*, 1:82–83.

3. *PNG*, 1:93.

4. Robert K. Wright Jr., *The Continental Army* (Washington, DC: Center of Military History, U.S. Army, 2000), 20.

5. *PNG*, 1:92.

6. *PNG*, 1:95.

7. *PNG*, 1:135.

8. *PNG*, 1:106.

9. On this, see Charles Royster, *A Revolutionary People at War: The Continental Army and American Character, 1775–1783* (Chapel Hill, NC: University of North Carolina Press, for the Institute of Early American History and Culture at Williamsburg, Virginia, 1980).

10. *PNG*, 1:160.

11. *PNG*, 1:194.

12. Theodore Thayer, *Nathanael Greene: Strategist of the American Revolution* (New York: Twayne, 1960), 67.
13. *PNG*, 1:173.
14. *PNG*, 1:119, 141, and 167.
15. *PNG*, 1:177.
16. *PNG*, 1:174.
17. *PNG*, 1:178.
18. *PNG*, 1:193.

Chapter Four: New York and New Jersey

1. *PNG*, 1:205.
2. Quoted in Christopher Ward, *The War of the Revolution*, ed. John Alden (New York: MacMillan, 1952), 1: 205.
3. *PNG*, 1:177.
4. Ward, *The War of the Revolution*, 206.
5. *PNG*, 1:225, 239.
6. *PNG*, 1:216.
7. *PNG*, 1:291–92.
8. James Thomas Flexner, *George Washington in the American Revolution* (Boston: Little, Brown, 1967), 119.
9. Edward G. Lengel, *General George Washington: A Military Life* (New York: Random House, 2005), 151–52.
10. Ward, *The War of the Revolution*, 238–51.
11. Thayer, *Nathanael Greene*, 112.
12. *PNG*, 1:311.
13. *PNG*, 1:342–43.
14. *PNG*, 1:344.
15. *The Writings of George Washington, from the Original Manuscript Sources, 1745–1799*, ed. John C. Fitzpatrick (Washington, DC: U.S. Government Printing Office, 1937), 6:285.
16. Lee to Washington, November 19, 1776, in *Papers of Charles Lee* (New York: New York Historical Society, 1872–1875), 2:286–88.
17. *PNG*, 1:352.
18. George F. Scheer and Hugh F. Rankin, *Rebels and Redcoats: The Living Story of the American Revolution* (Cleveland, OH: The World Publishing Co.,

1957), 210.

19. *PNG*, 1:368.
20. Quoted in Robert Leckie, *George Washington's War: The Saga of the American Revolution* (New York: HarperCollins, 1992), 296.
21. *PNG*, 1:370–72.
22. *PNG*, 2:7.

Chapter Five: The War in Pennsylvania: Brandywine and Germantown

1. *PNG*, 2:31.
2. G. W. Greene, *Life*, 338–39.
3. *PNG*, 2:47.
4. *PNG*, 2:87.
5. *PNG*, 2:50.
6. *PNG*, 2:99, 103.
7. *PNG*, 2:109.
8. *Journals of Congress: Containing Their Proceedings from January 1, 1777, to January 1, 1778, July 7, 1777* (Philadelphia: Folwell's Press, 1800), 3:223.
9. *PNG*, 2:111–14.
10. *PNG*, 2:140–41.
11. *PNG*, 2:149.
12. *PNG*, 2:162–63.
13. Thayer, *Nathanael Greene*, 196–97.
14. Leckie, *George Washington's War*, 458.
15. *PNG*, 10:379.
16. On these operations see John W. Jackson, *The Pennsylvania Navy, 1775–1782: The Defense of the Delaware* (New Brunswick, NJ: Rutgers University Press, 1994).
17. *PNG*, 2:202–3, 205.
18. *PNG*, 2:208–10.

Chapter Six: The Widened War

1. *PNG*, 2:231.
2. *PNG*, 2:260.

3. *PNG*, 2:260.
4. *PNG*, 2:260.
5. *PNG*, 2:285.
6. *PNG*, 2:307.
7. *PNG*, 2:326.
8. Thayer, *Nathanael Greene*, 227.
9. *PNG*, 2:277.
10. *PNG*, 2:301.
11. *PNG*, 2:439–40; Lengel, *General George Washington*, 291.
12. *PNG*, 2:446–47.
13. *PNG*, 2:461–63.
14. *PNG*, 2:464.
15. *PNG*, 2:530.
16. *PNG*, 3:223.
17. *PNG*, 3:412.
18. *PNG*, 3:429.
19. *PNG*, 4:323.
20. Joseph Plumb Martin, *Private Yankee Doodle: Being a Narrative of Some of the Adventures, Dangers and Sufferings of a Revolutionary Soldier,* ed. George F. Scheer (Boston: Little, Brown, 1962), 172.
21. *PNG*, 5:243.
22. *PNG*, 5:533.
23. *PNG*, 6:157.
24. *PNG*, 6:289.

Chapter Seven: The War in the South

1. *PNG*, 6:267.
2. *PNG*, 7:90.
3. *PNG*, 6:326.
4. *PNG*. 6:336.
5. *PNG*, 6:348–49.
6. *PNG*, 6:380.
7. *PNG*, 6:385.
8. *PNG*, 6:424.
9. *PNG*, 6:396.

10. *PNG*, 6:410.
11. *PNG*, 6:397–98.
12. *PNG*, 6:448.
13. *PNG*, 6:479.
14. *PNG*, 6:488–89.
15. Quoted in Robert Harvey, *A Few Bloody Noses*, 372.
16. *PNG*, 6:543.
17. *PNG*, 6:448.
18. *PNG*, 6:470.

Chapter Eight: Greene's Southern Campaign: First Phase

1. *PNG*, 7:19.
2. *PNG*, 7:111–12.
3. *PNG*, 7:9.
4. *PNG*, 7:106.
5. *PNG*, 7:188.
6. *PNG*, 7:225.
7. *PNG*, 7:268.
8. *PNG*, 7:266.
9. *PNG*, 7:363.
10. *PNG*, 7:287.
11. *PNG*, 7:287.
12. *PNG*, 7:287.
13. *PNG*, 7:293.
14. Scheer and Rankin, *Rebels and Redcoats*, 440.
15. *PNG*, 7:416.
16. *PNG*, 7:420.
17. *PNG*, 7:451.

Chapter Nine: Guilford Court House

1. *PNG*, 7324.
2. Henry Steele Commager and Richard B. Morris, eds., *The Spirit of Seventy-Six: The Story of the American Revolution as Told by Participants* (New York: Harper and Row, 1967), 1160.
3. *PNG*, 7:445.

4. Commager and Morris, *The Spirit of Seventy-Six*, 1168.
5. *PNG*, 7:481–82.

Chapter Ten: Hobkirk's Hill

1. *PNG*, 8:24.
2. *PNG*, 8:33.
3. *PNG*, 9:135.
4. *PNG*, 8:185.

Chapter Eleven: Fort Motte and Ninety Six

1. *PNG*, 8:350.
2. *PNG*, 8:300.
3. *PNG*, 9:36.

Chapter Twelve: Eutaw Springs

1. *PNG*, 9:41.
2. *The Writings of George Washington*, 22:146.
3. *PNG*, 9:329.
4. *PNG*, 9:332.
5. *PNG*, 9:358.
6. *PNG*, 8:64.
7. The obverse has a profile of Greene. On the reverse is a winged figure and the inscription in Latin, "The Safety of the Southern Department. The Foe conquered at Eutaw."
8. *PNG*, 9:362.

Chapter Thirteen: End of the War

1. *PNG*, 8:441.
2. *PNG*, 9:411–12.
3. *PNG*, 9:607.
4. *PNG*, 9:599–601.
5. *PNG*, 9:452.
6. *PNG*, 9:457.
7. *PNG*, 10:22.

8. *PNG*, 11:533.
9. *PNG*, 13:75.
10. John F. Stegman and James A. Stegman, *Caty: A Biography of Catherine Littlefield Greene* (Athens, GA: University of Georgia Press, 1977), 10.

Chapter Fourteen: Last Years

1 . Stegman and Stegman, *Caty*, 115.
2. *PNG*, 13:222.
3. Francis Vinton Greene, *General Greene* (New York: D. Appleton and Co., 1893), 309.
4. Ibid., 311–12.
5. *PNG*, 13:668.

Afterword

1. Henry Lee, *Memoirs of the War in the Southern Department of the United States* (New York: Inskeep and Bradford, 1812), 1:294.

SELECTED BIBLIOGRAPHY

Alden, John R. *The American Revolution, 1775–1783*. New York: Harper, 1954.

———. *The South in the Revolution, 1783–1789*. Baton Rouge, LA: Louisiana State University Press, 1957.

Alderman, Clifford Lindsey. *Retreat to Victory: The Life of Nathanael Greene*. Philadelphia: Clifton Books, 1967.

Anderson, Lee Patrick. *Forgotten Patriot: The Life and Times of Major-General Nathanael Greene*. N.p.: Universal Publishers, 2002.

Bailey, Ralph Edgar. *Guns over the Carolinas: The Story of Nathanael Greene*. New York: William Morrow and Co., 1967.

Bass, Robert D. *The Gamecock: The Life and Campaigns of General Thomas Sumter*. New York: Holt, Rinehard, and Winston, 1961.

———. *The Green Dragoon*. New York: Henry Holt and Co., Inc., 1957.

Bobrick, Benson. *Angel in the Whirlwind*. New York: Simon and Schuster, 1997.

Boyd, Thomas Alexander. *Light-Horse Harry Lee*. New York: Charles Scribner's Sons, 1931.

Buchanan, John. *The Road to Guilford Courthouse: The American Revolution in the Carolinas*. New York: John Wiley and Sons, 1997.

Callahan, North. *Henry Knox: General Washington's General*. New York: Rinehart and Co., Inc., 1958.

Clarke, Louise Brownell. *The Greenes of Rhode Island: With Historical Records of English Ancestry, 1534–1902*. New York: Knickerbocker Press, 1903.

Commager, Henry Steele, and Richard B. Morris, eds. *The Spirit of Seventy-Six: The Story of the American Revolution as Told by Participants*. New York: Harper and Row, 1967.

Davis, Burke. *Cowpens-Guilford Courthouse Campaign*. Philadelphia: J. B. Lippincott Co., 1962.

———. *Heroes of the American Revolution*. New York: Random House, 1971.

Edgar, Walter B. *Partisans and Redcoats: The American Revolution in the South Carolina Backcountry*. New York: Morrow, 2001.

Golway, Terry. *Washington's General: Nathanael Greene and the Triumph of the American Revolution*. New York: Henry Holt and Co., 2005.

Greene, Francis Vinton. *General Greene*. The Great Commander Series. New York: D. Appleton and Co., 1893.

Greene, George Washington. *The Life of Nathanael Greene, Major-General in the Army of the Revolution*. Vol. 1. New York: G. P. Putnam's Sons, 1867. Vols. 2 and 3. New York: Hard and Houghton, Riverside Press, 1871.

Greene, Nathanael. *The Papers of General Nathanael Greene*. 13 vols. Chapel Hill, NC: University of North Carolina Press for the Rhode Island Historical Society, 1976–2005.

Harvey, Robert. *A Few Bloody Noses: The Realities and Mythologies of the American Revolution*. New York: Overlook Press, 2001.

Leckie, Robert. *George Washington's War: The Saga of the American Revolution*. New York: HarperCollins, 1992.

Lee, Charles. *Papers of Charles Lee*. 2 vols. New York: New York Historical Society, 1872-75.

Lee, Henry. *Memoirs of the War in the Southern Department of the United States*. 2 vols. New York: Inskeep and Bradford, 1812.

Lengel, Edward G. *General George Washington: A Military Life*. New York: Random House, 2005.

Mackesy, Piers. *The War for America, 1775–1783*. Cambridge, MA: Harvard University Press, 1964.

Martin, Joseph Plumb. *Private Yankee Doodle: Being a Narrative of Some of the*

Adventures, Dangers and Sufferings of a Revolutionary Soldier. Edited by George F. Scheer. Boston: Little, Brown, 1962.

Meltzer, Milton, ed. *The American Revolutionaries: A History in Their Own Words.* New York: Harper Torch, 1993.

Morrill, Dan L. *Southern Campaigns of the American Revolution.* Mount Pleasant, SC: The Nautical & Aviation Publishing Company of America, 1993.

Pratt, Fletcher. "Nathanael Greene: The Quaker Turenne." First chapter of *Eleven Generals: Studies in American Command.* New York: William Sloane Associates, 1949.

Scheer, George F., and Hugh F. Rankin. *Rebels and Redcoats: The Living Story of the American Revolution.* Cleveland, OH: The World Publishing Co., 1957.

Simister, Florence Parker. *The Fire's Center: Rhode Island in the Revolutionary Era, 1763–1790.* Providence, RI: Rhode Island Bicentennial Foundation, 1979.

Simms, W. Gilmore. *The Life of Nathanael Greene, Major-General in the Army of the Revolution.* Philadelphia: Leary & Getz, 1849.

Siry, Steven E. *Greene: Revolutionary General.* Washington, DC: Potomac Books, 2007.

Stegman, John F., and James A. Stegman. *Caty: A Biography of Catherine Littlefield Greene.* Athens, GA: University of Georgia Press, 1977.

Thane, Elswyth. *The Fighting Quaker: Nathanael Greene.* New York: Hawthorn Books, 1972.

Thayer, Theodore. "Nathanael Greene: Revolutionary War Strategist." In *George Washington's Generals*, edited by George Athan Billias, 109–36. New York: William Morrow and Co., Inc., 1964.

———. *Nathanael Greene: Strategist of the American Revolution.* New York: Twayne, 1960.

Treacy, M. F. P*relude to Yorktown: The Southern Campaign of Nathaniel Greene, 1780–1781.* Chapel Hill, NC: University of North Carolina Press, 1963.

Ward, Christopher. *The War of the Revolution.* Edited by John Richard Alden. 2 vols. New York: The Macmillan Co., 1952.

Weigley, Russell F. *The Partisan War in the South: The South Carolina Campaign of 1780-1782.* Columbia, SC: University of South Carolina Press, 1970.

Willcox, William B. *Portrait of a General: Sir Henry Clinton in the War of Independence.* New York: Alfred A. Knopf, Inc., 1964.

INDEX

ABOUT THE AUTHOR

SPENCER C. TUCKER has written or edited thirty books on military and naval history. He is the recipient of two John Lyman Awards from the North American Society for Oceanic History for best books in naval history, the Theodore Roosevelt and Franklin Roosevelt Award for best book in naval history in 2004 for his biography of Captain Stephen Decatur, Jr., and his five-volume encyclopedia of the Cold War won the 2008 Society of Military History Award for best reference work. He taught for thirty years at Texas Christian University before holding for six years the John Biggs Chair in Military History at the Virginia Military Institute.